Let's Take a Walk

Written by:

Gina K. Trehus

For my family:

Mom, Cindy, Dad, Dewey, and my sister, Kayla, Grandma, and all my uncles, aunts, cousins, nieces, and nephews.

And for those who are no longer here with me, thank you for being part of my life. Until we meet on the other side, I will always hold a special place for you in my heart, and remember it's never goodbye, but always see you later.

For my best friends who were always there for me,

Thank you for being there when I needed you the most! I love you all!

Contents

Chapter 1

One summer weekend in July, our parents took us to the park so we could play. We arrived at the park around 9 a.m. so we could avoid the afternoon heat. Our parents took my sister and me over to the swings right away because my sister (Isabella) and I loved to swing. Of course, some other kids were over by the slide being mean to each other. They were calling each other names and pushing one another off the slide. Our parents never approved of this kind of behavior in the home, but they let us stay and play for a while. Then, around 11 a.m., our parents gathered us up at the park and told us it was time to go home and have lunch. So, we all went home.

After we returned home from the park, Dad grilled hot dogs and hamburgers for all of us while my sister and I built sandcastles in the sandbox our father had made for us. He called us up to the deck when the food was done, and we all sat around our deck dining table with an umbrella over our heads to eat. We got to eat outside, as the weather that day was a little hot but perfect under the umbrella. After we were finished eating, we all sat on the deck talking about the weather and what we wanted to be when we grew up.

I wanted to be an astronaut, and Isabella wanted to own her own business one day. After that, Dad called me over to sit on his lap when he asked me (at the age of eight) to do an exercise with him. He asked me to take a piece of paper and crumple it up, stomp on it, and really make a mess out of it, but to be careful not to rip it. Then I unfolded the piece of paper, smoothed it out, and he told me to look at how crinkled and dirty it was. He then told me to say sorry to the piece of paper. I refused at first because I didn't really see the point of apologizing, but he pointed out all the scars I had created and left behind, and that those scars would never go away no matter how hard I tried to fix it. He then said, "This is what happens if you ever bully another kid. No matter how much you apologize and say sorry, those scars will always stay there. They can never be erased." This is how we were taught to be nice to other children. No matter how rotten they can be toward you, you must treat them with respect and be kind to them.

At the age of 8, grandpa got a computer. My grandpa James Dome was the first one in our family to own one. Curious about how we would do with a computer, our parents took us down to our grandparents' house so we could play learning games on it. Grandpa showed us how to navigate and work on the computer first. Then he showed us what learning games we could play. It was mostly typing program games, but it was still fun. A year later, my dad's curiosity got the best of him. He started taking computers apart and building them back up. This time, he got me involved. Dad would build them, and I would program them. I think that's why I went into web design programming when I was older, but as a child, I really enjoyed programming. As the days flew by, summer was over, and we started school again.

I met a lot of friends throughout elementary and junior high school, but I only had a few who meant a lot to me. There was Jess, Madeley, Emilay, and Irelaynd. I grew up with Jess and Madeley, and we were inseparable, just like sisters.

All three of our fathers (including mine) went to high school together. It was our destiny to be best friends, but it wasn't until after we became friends that we found out all of our fathers were friends too. It's kind of weird how that worked out, but all we knew was that we had our dads' sense of humor. I met them like this: My best friend Jess and I have been friends for over 18 years. I remember the day I met her like it was yesterday. I'll never forget it.

I was in the fifth grade. That day, our class was going on a swimming field trip, so we took an early recess. I saw her walking all by herself outside by the swings. During that recess, I didn't have anyone to play with, so I decided to go up to her and ask what her name was. It was really hard for me to make friends that year.

"Hi," I said, and she smiled back. "Hi."

"What is your name?" I asked.

"Jessica," she said softly and shyly.

"Well, Jessica, I'm Amalia Rose. Nice to meet you. Do you want to play with me?"

"Sure," she said.

So I asked her if she wanted to swing. She just nodded her head, so we walked over to the swings and had a swinging contest to see who could swing the highest. If we were swinging at the same time, we would always laugh and giggle and then try to swing faster than the other. As the years passed, our friendship grew stronger. I lived a few miles out of town, and she lived in town on the south side. If the weather started to get bad during the winter, I would always "camp" out at her house until the weather cleared up. If it didn't, I would stay there. Jessica wasn't the "skinniest" beanpole around either, but like my mom and dad always taught us, never judge anyone until you get to know them, because they can be the sweetest person you will ever meet, and that was the case with her. Jess had long red-brown hair down the middle of her back and the most freckled face I had ever seen. She was a little taller than me.

In the seventh grade, I met my other best friend, Madeley. She was about a head and a half taller than me, skinny, with dirty-blonde hair and the bluest eyes I had ever seen. She was the sweetest thing ever. She was Jess's best friend, and she introduced us to each other. It was the first day of school when I met her. We lined up to enter the junior high as the bell rang, girls on the right and boys on the left. The principal gave us a short speech, and then we all entered the junior high. The school consisted of only seventh- and eighth-graders. Madeley was the quiet girl in line who never talked and was very shy. I thought to myself, "I can be friends with you; we will mesh well together." So I walked over and introduced myself after Jess did and got her talking. It was the best decision I ever made because we are still best friends today. We shared stories, asked how each other was doing, and she even offered me a place to stay when the roads were bad and buses wouldn't run. She is a best friend I would hold on to even after high school.

There's a saying we had here: after you graduate, you truly know who your real friends are. Some move away and never talk to you again. Others stick around and talk to you every week. Then there are those who move away and still keep in touch. Don't get me wrong, it would be nice to talk to all your friends every day, but let's be honest: life gets crazy after you graduate. You become extremely busy.

High school was never easy for me. It was hard getting to know people, especially when you get teased and bullied a lot. I wasn't exactly the "skinniest" person around. I struggled through my classes and never really took them seriously because I didn't understand all the homework that was being assigned. That changed when I was assigned to the resource room. I kept thinking, "Great, one more thing for people to tease me about." My confidence was low. But I learned something important about myself, it wasn't because I was dumb, like I thought. It was because I learned differently than others. I would overthink questions and homework. The resource room helped me a lot, and I would never take that experience back.

During my senior year of high school, I started having problems with my asthma, with repeated attacks at home and at school. My parents took me to our family doctor, who suggested I try a sport. The first thing I tried was soccer, but my asthma wouldn't cooperate, and I ended up sitting out more than playing. The second thing I tried was volleyball, but again, my asthma got in the way. I became very frustrated and felt like there was no hope with this endless medical condition.

My parents knew I loved martial arts and decided to try that instead. It was the best decision they ever made for me. My asthma attacks happened less and less, and my parents noticed a huge difference. Madeley was interested too and joined me. Jessie was interested as well, but after seeing what we were doing, she decided to cheer us on and take pictures instead. To this day, it's something I've stuck with, along with softball.

Softball was another passion of mine. I've been playing since I was three, and when I turned 15, I played for the Junior Olympic team here in town. We were undefeated and placed first. I met a lot of friends that year. Unfortunately, when you turn 17 during the season, you're unable to play with that team anymore. Now, I am a pitcher for our all-women's team, and I love it. Last year, we were rec three champs.

As time passed and our senior year flew by, graduation arrived. It was a time of tears and proud moments, not goodbyes, but "see you laters." Most of us moved on to college and started completely new chapters in our lives.

After the graduation ceremony and party were over, I went into the backyard and stood on the back porch, leaning against the railing and letting the warm summer breeze blow through my hair as I reflected on what I wanted to do in college.

As I stood there on the back porch, letting the warm summer breeze blow through my hair, I thought about what I really loved and who I wanted to be. Even as a kid, I had always been drawn to the storms, the wind, the lightning, the raw power of nature. That curiosity never left me. By the time I was in high school, I became trained in Skywarn, the volunteer program with the National Weather Service. I chased tornadoes, not recklessly, but with a love for understanding them, documenting them, and keeping people safe. I guess it was my way of chasing something bigger than myself, something I could control even when the world seemed unpredictable.

It was a little nerve-wracking at times, wondering if I was good enough, if I could handle it all, if my work mattered. Half my life, I had been told I wasn't good enough, and sometimes that voice still lingered in the back of my mind. But I chased the storms anyway, because it was who I was, and no one could take that from me.

Chapter 2

College… it was something I just wasn't looking forward to. High school was hard enough for me, always getting teased, and I was not looking forward to the whole idea of having your schedule set and planned out for you. It just wasn't something I wanted in my life. I wanted to work for a year, save up, and then go out to California and go to college there. That was my dream and what I wanted.

Unfortunately, that summer I had to go out to a friend of the family's farm and help watch her kids for the month of July. It was out in Thief River, MN. Her name was Brailey Jones; my mom went to high school with her. They needed a babysitter while they worked out in the fields from sunup to sundown. Her eldest daughter, Duncan, was going to summer school, so she was unable to watch her little brother, Colton Jones, and little sister, Tadley Jones, while they worked. They provided me with a roof over my head so I didn't have to drive back and forth from a hotel clear out to the country, and they provided food for me to eat, which cut down on costs. Duncan and I got along and tolerated each other, so it wasn't complete torture staying with the family.

I planned on signing up for college when I came back into town. I wanted to go to college in California because they have an awesome softball program out there, and that's where I wanted to play. But when I came back to town, I had another thing coming. My parents signed me up for college while I was gone. I was very, very angry about what they had done. I mean, it was a community college, so it wasn't all that bad, but it wasn't what I wanted. I did not want to go there at all. I tried fighting for what I wanted, but they had already submitted the paperwork to get grants through the programs they had there, and I was already accepted, so it was a lose-lose situation.

For my parents' peace of mind, even though I was 100% against it, I met with a school counselor, you know, one of those people who helps you get signed up for the degree you want to go into. I first chose computer science, but that lasted a whole six months. It was just way too complicated and hard for me. So I decided to go into information processing. I guess I was okay with going to school there; I didn't really have a choice. So I decided to give it a try. After all, what would it hurt, right?

I still really wanted to go to California, and I just couldn't drop the subject. My parents continued to argue that if I moved away to another state, they would not help me with money or anything like that. They would have disowned me and cut me off from everything. I didn't know if I would have been able to make it on my own, so I had to adjust to the community college my parents signed me up for.

My first day of school went great, and I knew from that point on I was going to love it. I took my general classes, and then I took choir. I had taken choir in high school with my two best friends, Jess and Madeley, and decided to take it again in college. On the first day of class, I met Emilay. She was a tall lady, very pretty, with long sandy blonde hair and blue eyes. Her personality was like you wouldn't believe, sassy, smart, with a great sense of humor, and very confident. We also took vocal lessons together, and from there our friendship kicked off and we grew closer.

Emilay's voice was so pretty; it was like an angel singing. We'd always make her sing, volunteering her for talent shows and solos when we were out in public. It was very entertaining and made the time go by faster when there wasn't anything to do around campus. But man, if you got the two of us in the same room, it created trouble sometimes. We would feed off each other's energy and find some way to get ourselves into trouble. It always gave us something to talk about.

We'd be cracking jokes left and right, and every Friday night we would have a rock band night, make chocolate chip cookies, and drink milk at her house with her boyfriend, Sam. We'd fight like sisters and then say, "Well, that was stupid of us to fight over that," and move on with our lives. It was never worth ending a friendship over. Honestly, we had made it this far in our lives being friends, why throw it away over something stupid?

The next day rolled around, and my first class was general math. That's when I met Ellie. She was as tall as me, skinny, with short blonde hair and blue eyes, but she was ten years older than me. She was a young whippersnapper with a sassy, sweet side and very independent. The day I met her, I was the only one sitting at the tables we had in class. She walked over to me and said, "Is this spot open? I don't feel like sitting at the other tables, and I noticed you were sitting by yourself."

I have to admit, it was the first day of math class, and I was a little shy and bashful. "No, this spot is not taken, and yes, you can sit here, no harm done," I replied. And our friendship took off from there. We would talk about the weather and about our animals. She had two cats, and we had one cat and two dogs. We would show pictures to each other until class started. We loved our animals just like our children!

Then the bell rang, and math class started. The teacher began with a "Good morning, students," and we said it back. He wrote a few math problems on the board and asked us to solve them. We worked for about a half hour.

"Okay, students, who has the answer to the first problem?" he said. No one raised their hand. I looked around for a few seconds, then raised my hand until he called on me, and I gave him the answer.

"Very good, Amalia."

"Okay, class, who knows the answer to the second problem?" he asked. Again, no one raised their hand, so I answered the question.

"Again, very good, Amalia," he said, and wrote the first two answers on the board.

Then he asked the third question. "Class, who has the answer to the third problem?" No one answered, so again I raised my hand. He looked at me and said, "Amalia, no more answering questions. You need to give the other classmates a chance."

So I sat there patiently as he asked another question. And who do you think answered it? No one. So I slowly raised my hand.

"Okay, Amalia, go ahead and answer the question."

So I did. Ellie just rolled her eyes at me and started laughing. I couldn't help it, I liked answering math questions.

Then there was Irelaynd. She was a few years younger than me. I met her through the women's softball league I played on. She's an outstanding person in general and one heck of an outfielder, one of my favorites! She has a bubbly personality, is very easygoing, and very outgoing.

The semester went fast, and before you knew it, it was time to graduate from college. We all graduated in December, except for Irelaynd. She entered college right after I graduated. We were all having problems finding jobs in our hometown, so we decided to move to California. I already had another friend staying there. Her name was Lilly; she was my mom's friend's daughter. She was a model for an agency, a little taller than me, with blonde hair, blue eyes, and just drop-dead gorgeous.

I called her one night and told her we were having trouble finding jobs. She suggested we move to California and move in with her. She didn't mind at all; she was excited for us to stay. It was really weird, in a good way. There were no catfights, no arguing, nothing. We each had our own separate schedules.

At the beginning of the year, we all agreed to save up our money and go on vacation to Hawaii. Irelaynd took the year off to figure out what degree she wanted to go into, but she did go on the trip with us. We each found jobs five months after graduating. It was extremely hard work, but we did it., Jess worked at an art institute, Madeley opened her own daycare facility, which I worked at too, Emilay worked at a career center, and Irelaynd worked at a grooming facility for dogs and cats. It took us three years to save up, but finally we were able to go.

We stayed in Waikiki. The beach was beautiful and amazing. Warm ocean breeze, sand in between my toes, and the touring was the best part! We had a person we didn't know take our picture. I made copies of the picture, framed it, and gave it to Jess, Madeley, Emilay, Ellie, and Irelaynd. We were the six musketeers, inseparable. It was just an awesome time.

We were only in Hawaii for seventeen days. We surfed and rode the waves, toured, went on zip lines, played mini golf, did an underwater submarine, attended luaus, and went shopping, my favorite. Well, surfing was a favorite too, but who doesn't like to shop! We got to scuba dive in the clear waters and went on hikes. The seventeen days soon came and went, and before we knew it, it was time to go back to California. I wasn't a fan of going back; it was just so beautiful there. So we packed up our things and got ready to fly home. When we got home, we returned to our normal lives.

Years passed down the road, and we weren't getting any younger, so we all decided to have a ladies' night out and go to this club in town called Club Phero. It was the hottest club in town, and we loved going there. They played all different types of music and had a lot of different drinks. I had no intention of meeting anyone that night.

Before we went out, Emilay, Irelaynd, Jess, Ellie, and Madeley all came over to my house, and we got ready for the night out. We cranked the music up and jammed out to our favorite songs on a CD we had put together the night before. It was really nice to just jam and forget about all my worries.

Of course, to make the night more interesting, before we went out, Jess and Madeley hid in the coat closet to scare Emilay and Irelaynd. Ellie knew what was going on. She walked right past them and saw them. She just looked at them, laughed, and rolled her eyes. She's lucky none of the other girls heard her laugh. Those two are the biggest pranksters of them all, but I love every minute of it. Why not make life more interesting than it already is, right?

Before those two knuckleheads went into the closet, I grabbed my jacket and placed it in my room. Jess and Madeley were done getting ready way before all of us.

Right before we left, Emilay and Irelaynd were looking for Jess and Madeley. "Amalia, where are Jess and Madeley?" they both said at the same time. "Ummmm, I think they went out to the car already. Grab your jacket and meet me out there, it's cool and windy out," I said to them.

As Emilay and Irelaynd opened the closet door, Jess and Madeley jumped out and scared the crap out of them. It was hysterical. "Oh, Emilay, you should have seen your face, and you too, Irelaynd. It was priceless. Thank goodness for video cameras, because I got that one recorded," I told the girls.

They weren't too thrilled about the prank or about us knowing what they were planning, but we sure fooled them. "Come on now, you have to admit you knew something was up when you couldn't find Jess and Madeley," I said to them. "Yes, I figured something was up, but I couldn't pin down what was going on. I had no idea those two would jump out of a closet," Emilay said. "I must admit, you two, that was an awesome prank you pulled on us. But don't worry, someday, when you're not expecting it, we'll get you back," Irelaynd said. "Yes, because we all know you can't pull a prank with that not-so-straight face you try on us all the time," I said to Irelaynd.

She just looked at me and started cracking a smile. "See, you can't even keep a straight face when I look at you. But don't worry, I still love you," I said to her. "Yeah, yeah, yeah, I know, I know. I was only kidding," Irelaynd said. "Okay, let's go, ladies. We don't want to waste the night away standing here. Let's get out there and have some fun tonight," I said to all of them.

We went to a couple of different clubs, danced the night away, and had an amazing time. It was a much-needed night out with the girls. We had Jess's sister, Tayla, give us a ride all over town as our DD (designated driver). She had just turned 21. She drove to my house and left her car there, then took Jess's vehicle since it had more room.

We told her she could bring a friend if she wanted, but she opted to hang out with us instead, which was fine because we all get along great together. All in all, we had an amazing time.

Since I had a house on the outskirts of town, Tayla dropped everyone off at my place, and they all spent the night there. She then got in her vehicle and went home. Before she left, we each gave her fifty dollars as a thank-you for being our DD that night. After all, who would want to drive around a bunch of tanked-up ladies who'd had one too many drinks? In the end, though, she did enjoy driving us around. There was no fighting or bickering going on at that moment.

Before she left, I told her, "Tayla, please call me when you get home so I know you made it home safe. There are too many weirdos out at this time of night." Forty-five minutes later, she called me. "Mali, I made it home safe. I'm going to bed now," Tayla said. "Okay, thank you for calling me. Have a good night, and thanks again for driving us home," I said to her. "You're welcome. Good night. Bye," Tayla said, and she hung up the phone.

I looked around, and everyone was sleeping. "Well, that didn't take long," I said to myself.

I took a shower, put my PJs on, and went to bed.

In the morning, we all got up around noon-ish. We were all hungover and tired. "Good afternoon, ladies," I said to them.

All I could hear was grumbling and mumbling. It was kind of funny, but I was hungover too from one too many drinks. "Last night was an amazing night, and I had so much fun," I said to them.

They all just shook their heads. I gave them aspirin and coffee, pop, or juice, whatever they preferred. One by one, they all left for the day. Before they did, I said, "I just wanted to say thank you, ladies, for the amazing night out. It was sooooo much fun!"

They all started talking at once, and all I heard was, "I had a lot of fun," "Oh, you're welcome," and "We need to have one of these nights every month." I believe Jess said that last one, and we all started to laugh.

They all left within ten minutes of each other. After they left, I laid back down for the rest of the day, as my head was pounding and my stomach was twirling. But I have to admit, it was a pretty amazing night, and I would do it all over again if I could. I just couldn't wait until next month to have another ladies' night out.

Chapter 3

I used to be something in my life, a martial arts instructor, a gymnastics coach, a softball player, and a database technician who enrolled students in classes and did money reports for the college I had worked for back home.

I remember how good that felt. I started to stare off into space, recalling the memories I had. I was smiling and laughing at them until one day, my life changed. I never knew how important it was to pay attention to the small details in a person's life and job. Boy, did I learn my lesson that day.

I got up and started my day like I did any other morning. I got up at 6 a.m., took a shower, put my pajamas back on, brushed my hair, brushed my teeth, got my breakfast and lunch ready, put my work clothes on, and went to work.

When I walked into work that morning, I was immediately pulled into my boss's office. She asked me to sit down. All I could think was, *Man, this is not good.* She turned to close the door, walked over to his desk, and sat down. She explained the few mistakes I had made, simple spelling errors, and math mistakes. But the thing that got me was that my math was always double-checked by her, so I feel like I was set up for failure before I even helped her out. I got accused by the college of stealing money, my bank accounts were combed through, and I lost my job because of this. She told me she couldn't afford to have mistakes like this made for the college. Then she looked at me point-blank and said, "I'm sorry, but I'm going to have to let you go. Please pack up your things at your desk and leave the office immediately."

I was so ashamed of myself. I should have known better. Better than helping her out. It was just a few honest mistakes. Could she do that? Fire me because of this? I was never told about these mistakes. How was I supposed to know I made them if no one told me? It didn't make sense. Were they trying to get rid of me because they didn't like me? I just kept thinking to myself, it was just a simple mistake. Just an honest and simple mistake. I mean, really… no one is perfect. No one. No matter how hard you try to be perfect, no one really is.

She asked me to go to my desk, pack everything up, and leave as soon as I could. "You're not welcome here anymore," she said. I didn't even get a chance to explain myself, and she didn't even think about giving me a second chance.

I gave her a nod, tears running down my face, turned around, opened her office door, and walked out. I thought about slamming the door shut, but decided it wouldn't be very professional. I walked straight to my desk and started packing up my things. As I packed, I looked at each item carefully, recalling the memories tied to it, as if it were the last time I would ever see it.

I wiped my eye and looked to my right. There was a framed photo of my close friends and me from a Christmas party we had thrown together. I continued packing my pictures and little trinkets, the things that made the office feel like a second home. Before I knew it, everything at my desk was packed up.

I said my final goodbyes and "see you laters" to everyone I knew and had become friends with at the office. Then I put everything into my car and went home. I stood outside my house for a while, pondering what I would do with my life now that I didn't have a job. After a few minutes, I got cold, so I grabbed my things from the car, carried them to the front door, unlocked it, walked inside, set my stuff down in the entryway, and sat on the couch, just staring off into space, looking out the window, wondering what I would do from here.

I was so ashamed of myself. I couldn't believe what had just happened. I worked so hard to get where I was, and now my job, everything I had worked for, was gone, just like that. It was a complete shock. Not in a million years did I think I would be in this position.

I sat there thinking, *how am I going to pay my bills? How am I going to afford everyday living expenses while I don't have a job?* Things needed to change. First, I thought about fixing my mistakes. I knew it wouldn't help to go back to my employer,

But soon after I started to lay in bed, my curiosity grew, which then began to turn into worry, and worry grew into anxiety, and anxiety grew into fear. This was not a good combo, and I knew I was in for a long night and a long haul. Not that it would matter at all, after all, what did I really have planned for tomorrow, right? Man, did I have a rude awakening coming for me. So I ended up tossing and turning most of the night.

After a full night of tossing and turning, nightmare after nightmare, I gave up on sleeping, and with so much going on inside my head, I decided it would be best for me to take a walk downtown to my best friend Jessica's house from the place where I lived (which was just on the outskirts of town). It was just before the sun came up. I had a couple of miles to walk to town, so by the time I reached my friend's house, it would be daylight. After all, not having a job to pay for gas, I had to think of ways to save money. Besides, walking wasn't all that bad for you; I was getting my exercise in for the day, that's for sure.

Businesses opened up in town right before the sun came up, around 7 a.m. I knew my best friend would be up by then, so I didn't have to worry about waking her up. She was always up at the crack of dawn (I never did understand how she could be an early riser. After all, you would have to take the jaws of life to get me out of bed. I could never get up that early). I just needed a friend to talk to and someone to hang out with for a little bit, and

I knew I could count on her for that.

It was only in the upper 40s that morning, so it was a little cool out. I grabbed a jacket and put it on as I walked out of the house. "Brrrrr, it's a little chilly out this morning," I said as I zipped up my jacket. The air was fresh, crystal clear, and smelled of morning dew, and the sky was just turning from night to morning. I could barely spot the stars as the sun began to peek above the horizon. I stopped at the end of my driveway and looked up at the stars I could barely see for a few minutes.

"They are so beautiful. Sometimes we just don't take the time to appreciate what we have in front of us," I whispered to myself. As a kid, our parents would let us camp out in the backyard. This fresh air reminded me of the memories of sitting in the tent, listening to the birds sing, and smelling the fresh morning dew.

So, on my long walk to town, I decided to wander a little bit off the road. The first half mile of the road was straight uphill, and the trees grew together over the top of it, making a tunnel of leaves in the summer, a tunnel of snow in winter, and a tent of bare branches like charred fingers the rest of the year. Across the road, I saw a ditch full of cattails and the clearing of a field full of corn, stretching out green and smooth, then disappearing over a slope into a rolling sea of hills full of wheat and barley. I could also see the meadowlarks flying in and out of the ditches and fields.

As I stopped and stared at them, I started to ponder a few things I just couldn't stop thinking about. If I was going to survive this new path of life I was on, I had to try to clear the emotions and thoughts that had been going through my head all day. I know… I know… sometimes pondering can be dangerous to a person's well-being, especially for me of all people. Speaking of pondering and wondering, I had no idea what part of town I had walked into.

I looked down where I was walking, not paying close attention to where I was going. I came across an abandoned building on the outskirts of town. There were rotting floorboards with scattered broken glass, rusted screws and bolts, and pieces of flattened iron that used to be part of something bigger a long time ago.

I heard a little scuffle and two ladies yelling at an older gentleman above where I was walking. I walked over a few feet under the boards from where the ladies were standing and looked through the cracks of the broken boards near the top of the stairs. I saw the two ladies and then a man weeping for his life. I could see one lady holding a gun on him. The man yelled, "No… no… please don't… I didn't mean it… please… please, I'm begging you."

All of a sudden, I froze in my tracks and ducked behind the staircase so they wouldn't notice me.

I looked up at the two ladies, and all of a sudden, boom, I heard a gunshot. They had shot the trembling, scared man. I heard one of the ladies shout, "You should have thought of that earlier," and the other one was laughing. They thought it was funny to shoot someone. I couldn't believe my own eyes. It was very heartless of them. I had no idea what they were talking about; I thought it was money at first, or it could have been a deal-gone-bad situation.

I came out from under the stairs and lost my footing as I started to walk backward. Not watching where I was going, I ended up tripping over my clumsy feet and onto a not-so-steady board. I fell backward through the broken wood on the second floor and dropped twelve feet to the ground floor. That knocked the wind right out of me. I laid on the ground for about thirty seconds, trying to gasp for air, which felt like an eternity.

I heard the two ladies scuffle their feet above me and then heard them run down the stairs. Then I looked up at the empty floor I had just fallen through. "Ouch, that hurt," I whispered, rubbing my back and looking again at the hole above me. Out of the corner of my eye, I spotted the two ladies who shot the man looking down at me. The crash was so loud they had heard it from the second floor.

"Erika, look," said Becky, pointing down at me.

"Becky, let's go get her," said Erika.

"Great, now what?" I thought to myself as panic set in. My heart was pounding so loud and fast, I felt like it was going to beat right out of my chest. I ran hopelessly into a neighborhood I had never been in before and found a bookshop built like a house with a huge glass window you could see in and out of. There was a sign on top in rainbow colors that read My Teacakes Brookhouse. You could get hot and cold tea, coffee, cupcakes, and cakes. Inside were oodles and oodles of bookshelves filled with books.

My mother and father took us here when I was a young teenager. I'll never forget it, we used to go here every Sunday after church. It was our family time together. I loved how it smelled, like chocolate, cake, and coffee.

On the outside of the house was a front deck with tables and chairs for people to sit and read any type of material they liked while enjoying a snack and a beverage. Next to the window were four black metal stands holding newspapers and magazines, each about four and a half feet tall. Beside the deck was a row of orange and blue daylilies and yellow and purple tulips.

It was already 7 a.m., and the bookhouse was open. I decided to go inside, thinking those ladies would never find me there. It was a safe place, right? I mean, why would two women who just shot someone go into a bookhouse looking for me? I figured it would be the last place they'd ever search.

Well, my curiosity definitely got the best of me. As I stood by the big window looking outside, I saw Erika and Becky walking up the block with guns in their hands, searching frantically. They passed a white house as a man stepped outside. As soon as he saw them, he turned around, went back inside, and called the police.

As the ladies looked around, they both spotted me standing by the window.

"Erika, there she is," said Becky.

"Okay, let's go get her," said Erika.

I had nowhere to run, they were way too close. Instead, I saw a good hiding spot behind a bookshelf in the corner. "They'll never find me here," I whispered.

The ladies came charging into the bookhouse like they owned the place, screaming, "I know you're here. Come out… come out… wherever you are." I knelt in the corner, shaking and trembling so badly I was scared out of my wits. I put my hands over my mouth so I wouldn't make a sound.

I lost my footing again and bumped the bookshelf. Becky spotted me as it shifted.

"Come out, I know you're here," she shouted.

When I ignored her, she grew agitated.

"COME OUT! I KNOW YOU'RE HERE!"

I decided to do the right thing and came out from behind the shelf.

"I know what you saw, little girl," Becky said.

"Don't call me a little girl. I didn't see anything, it was just a figment of my imagination," I said with a small chuckle. "Besides, it was dark out," I added snobbishly.

Becky got in my face, grabbed my shirt, and pointed the gun under my chin.

"I know what you saw. Admit it. We saw you, and you saw us."

Seeing how agitated she was getting, I decided to lie some more. I told her I hadn't seen anything, that she had the wrong person, and that I was just exploring the building before it was torn down while walking to my friend's house. I had so much on my mind, I needed a long walk.

Knowing I wasn't going to make it to my friend's house, I had to think of a way out. I struggled away and hid behind the same bookshelf again, which only made Becky angrier. She grabbed a customer ordering a cupcake and tea and held the gun to them.

"Come out, or this one won't survive," she said.

"Okay, I'll come out if you let her go and have her sit down," I said. She agreed. I needed to stall, it was my only option to survive.

I stepped into the open and stood in front of the window. Becky raised the gun, and I stared straight into the barrel.

"No wonder I heard the gunshot and saw the muzzle flash, she didn't have a suppressor," I said softly.

She pulled the trigger. I saw the bullet coming and somehow moved just in time. It missed me by milliseconds, shattered the window behind me, and sent glass flying into the magazine rack.

"SWEET!" I told myself.

Becky and Erika stood there with their mouths open.

"How did you do that?" Becky asked.

"Do what?" I smirked.

"Move out of the way so I couldn't shoot you?" Erika said.

"I don't know how I did it," I replied, "but you have to admit, it was pretty cool."

Chapter 4

By then, the sheriff just so happened to be driving by, and at that moment the call went out to all officers. He was the one who ended up taking the call that one of the neighbors had phoned in. He approached the bookhouse slowly and cautiously, with his gun in his hand. He walked up slowly to the front deck area of the bookhouse and started to yell at me.

"Excuse me, miss, what is your name?"

"Amalia Rose," I replied back to him. "What's yours?"

"Nikoli," replied the sheriff. "Please walk slowly backward to me, away from the two ladies with the gun."

As I tried to take some steps backward toward the sheriff, Becky once again raised her gun at me and aimed it at my head, and Erika raised hers at the sheriff.

"Take another step and I'll attempt another shot at you," said Becky.

I looked at her and then turned to look at Erika and noticed Erika had her gun pointed at the sheriff. So, I froze in my steps and attempted to bargain for the other people who were stuck in the bookhouse with me.

"How about I stay here and you let the others go? It's me you want, not them," I said.

Becky stood there for a second as she stared fearlessly into the sheriff's eyes. The sheriff nodded at the two ladies, letting them know the deal would be legit. Becky and Erika looked at each other and both agreed to let the other hostages go.

So, the sheriff put his gun back in his safety holster and moved all four black metal stands out of the way from where the glass window used to be so that the hostages could use that as an escape route, because Erika was guarding the main door and refused to get out of their way. After all the hostages were let go, the sheriff took the magazine racks and set them in the spot where the window used to be, next to each other, creating yet another barrier.

So it's just Becky, Erika, and me. I'm looking at these magazine/newspaper racks that are stacked beside each other, and I start racking up a crazy idea. I could use these like stairs or like a ladder. But with the sheriff on the other side, I decided to sit on the floor. I began staring back and forth at the magazine racks, the sheriff, and the ladies.

Then I plotted a plan in my head, not a smart one, but one that just came to me at a moment's notice. I decided I was going to take a run at the stands and climb up them. There was enough room on top for me to squeeze through, but the first attempt was a complete failure. I slipped and got my shoe stuck, and not only that, Becky pulled me off while I was hanging on and threw me onto the ground like a piece of trash. My shoe never came with me; it was stuck in the rack.

I took one heck of a nasty spill and scraped up my knee.

"Ow, that hurt, you bonehead!" I shouted to Becky, and she started to laugh.

"Can I go get my shoe and put it back on, please?" Becky just rolled her eyes and said, "Go ahead."

I limped over to the magazine rack and got my shoe unstuck. I put it back on, and just as I turned around, I saw Becky looking at me and starting to laugh the words, "Oh, my bad," and then she turned to give Erika a high five.

In the midst of the two of them giving each other a high five, they were both distracted. I took advantage of the situation. I looked closely at the two of them and noticed that both of them had their guns to their sides. If I was going to break free, now would be the time to do it.

Using my martial arts training, I decided to take control of the situation. I grabbed Erika's gun and elbowed her in the nose. She dropped her gun. I gripped it, threw it down, and then kicked the other gun out of Becky's hand.

Now I knew I was in for a ride. Now that I'd just done this, it didn't look good. I was going to have to defend myself. A fight broke out. Erika tried punching me, but I blocked it, grabbed her arm, broke her elbow, gave her an instant black eye, and broke her nose, as she was the one guarding the door. Erika was on the ground holding her face and nose with her other hand that wasn't broken.

Becky grabbed my hand and smiled. I smiled back, ripped my hand out of her grip, and punched her in the mouth and nose. I gave Becky a bloody lip and nose. She was the one who put up a good fight. It wasn't over yet. She fought back with a few punches and kicks. I finally grabbed her and threw her over my head into a bookshelf, and she went down. I knew I had her; she stood no chance against me!

After the first round, both ladies were on the floor for a few minutes.

"Looks like it's time for me to break free," I said to myself.

I ran toward the sheriff and yelled at him to move the magazine racks, but there was a problem, he couldn't. They were stuck. So, I had no option but to run up the rack, roll over the top of it, and jump off the front deck. I would have gone out the front door, but Becky threw the bookshelf in front of the door, so I had no choice but to take the magazine rack route.

Barely making it, I took a quick turn behind me and noticed that Becky and Erika were getting up and starting to run toward me. The sheriff grabbed my hand and said, "It's time to go. You need to start running."

So I took off with the sheriff, running to safety, and in the process, the police now had the building surrounded. Not only that, but for everyone's safety, they also had a two-block barrier. The sheriff quickly glanced behind us and saw a rack go flying across the yard.

"Well, that can't be good," I told the sheriff.

"Keep running. Don't look back. They are coming. We need to get to safety," the sheriff yelled at me.

"I'm going to get you no matter how fast you run!" Becky yelled at me.

Before I noticed, she knocked the sheriff over, and his gun went flying out of his hands. I stopped in my tracks, and now I was the only one standing, and she had the gun pointed at my head... again. I tried to run again, and she ended up tripping me. I went flying forward and fell on my face, hands, and knees. (As if I hadn't fallen enough today, right?)

Exhausted and out of breath, I decided to stay on the ground for a few seconds where it was safe. In the meantime, the cops surrounded Becky and me. Becky turned and pointed the gun at one of the cops, but the cops started yelling at her to put the gun down. She started staring at all the guns pointed at her and shortly realized that she had no chance against them, so she gave up.

She put her hands in the air. The cops gave her directions to turn around, interlock her fingers behind her head, and kneel on the ground. As I sat there and watched the cops arrest her, I decided I'd rested enough and got up off the ground.

I got up, wobbled a little as I was lightheaded, and stood still. In the distance, I heard a voice yelling at me to duck down because Erika was coming at me, but it was too late. By the time I tried ducking, Erika came up behind me and cracked me a good one behind the head and neck with her gun.

Again, I had an encounter with the ground, but this time I was gasping for air, not realizing if it was from being in too much pain or if I was just in shock. I fell to the ground, and as I was falling, I started to feel funny. I noticed something in the crowd, it looked like my best friend Jessica.

Oh, it is my best friend!! I thought to myself as the outside grew darker and darker. The darker my vision became, the more I struggled for air. I heard the cops arresting both Erika and Becky. Then I knew, I knew I was safe, and shortly thereafter, I fell asleep. But before I did, Erika and Becky spotted what I was looking at and gathered that I knew the person I was staring at in the crowd.

The sheriff called for an ambulance to transport me to the hospital to make sure I was OK. I woke up in the hospital and started to freak out. I didn't want them to find me. I started to scream, "Get me out of here! They are going to find me! Please come and help me!"

The doctors and nurses came rushing in to tell me where I was and that the rooms were heavily guarded so no one but them could get in. You even had to sign each time you came in and out of the room. I asked the doctor if I was going to be OK, and they said yes, but I had a concussion and would have to stay for a few days to be watched.

I kept asking for the sheriff at the hospital, but he didn't make it there. He was back at the bookhouse taking statements and talking to the witnesses, so I asked the doctors to relay a message to him that I was OK and only had a concussion. I tried to gather my things to leave, but the doctors wouldn't let me leave, nor would the protection detail the sheriff put outside the door.

Great. I couldn't leave. I just wanted to see my best friend.

But what I didn't know was that Jess had talked with the sheriff.

"Hey, Sheriff, come here, please," said Jess.

"Yes, how may I help you?"

"Do you know where they are taking Amalia to?" Jess said.

"Yes, they took her to the hospital down the road. You can ask admitting what room she's in there. You must have been the friend she was walking to earlier," the sheriff said.

"Yes, I am her best friend, Jess. She can never stay out of trouble. It just has a habit of finding her," Jess said.

"I'll call the hospital and let them know you're coming and put you on the list so you can go in and see her," the sheriff said.

"OK, thank you," Jess said.

I never did make it over to my friend's house that day, but you have to admit this is going to be one awesome story to tell her when I manage to get over to her place, which is funny to speak of. Guess who came rolling up to the hospital? You got it! My best friend Jess. I couldn't believe it!!

"Man, am I sooooo glad to see you, Jess," I said as she entered my room. She just looked at me, shook her head, and spoke. "You know, Amalia, I thought I'd find you here. Where trouble rolls, I shall find you right behind it."

Well, it's not my fault trouble seems to just cross my path… and then that's when I realized something. Becky and Erika saw me looking at Jess in the crowd. I couldn't help but think, are they going to hurt her if they ever get out of prison? Did I just do the wrong thing?

So I called in the security detail who were guarding my room and asked them to put us in protective custody. They told me the sheriff had already placed me in it and would be up at the hospital in a little bit. Phew! What a relief!

After an hour, the sheriff made it up to my room, and I sat and talked with him about the whole situation and how it happened. I begged him to place my friend and me in protective custody, as well as my family and everyone who was close to me. Before he left, I gave him a big hug and said my thank-yous. Without him there, I have no idea how that would have turned out.

I was only in the hospital for three days, and after that all my family and friends I knew were put into a protective custody program for eleven years, and we could move anywhere in the US we wanted. But we decided to move across the US. We picked out a spot where I grew up, back home, where we belonged, back home to Mandan, ND. After all, who would look there, right?

I felt a little guilty, though, because I couldn't stop thinking of Lilly. I was staying with her, and she was kind enough to open her home to me. I asked her to come with me, but of course Lilly stayed behind because ND did not have a modeling agency. However, she did come and visit a few times a year, which was OK. That way, we could keep up with each other besides our daily phone calls.

We did have a program on our computers that we could use to talk to each other. So every night at 9 pm, we would get on our computers and video chat for an hour or so, which was nice because that way we were able to keep in touch.

Chapter 5

This was a day I would regret, I just knew it. It was time to go to court to testify, hopefully to put Erika and Becky behind bars, where they belonged, once and for all. I didn't want to go in. The lawyer practically had to drag me into the courtroom while convincing me that it was safe. I looked at him and said, "Do you remember the last time I got tangled up with these two crazies? I ended up in the back of an ambulance because of them. I do not want to go down that route ever again."

"Mali, that's not going to happen. There are officers in there that will prevent that from happening. You are safe, I promise you," the lawyer spoke.

All I could think to myself was, *yeah, right.*

"You better get that ambulance ready because you're going to need it," I told the lawyer. He just giggled and grabbed my hand while walking me into the courtroom.

The court had opening statements for each side. The proceedings took four long, grueling days. On the first day, Erika had an outburst about how she wanted to kill me and that I would never see another day to live, because no matter where I was, she would find me. Well, the judge was not having any of that. He ordered the bailiff to drag her out of the courtroom. As the bailiff was putting handcuffs on her, she started kicking and yelling at unseen things. It took both the bailiff and the sheriff to get her into the holding cell.

"Are we really going to do this again, Erika?" the sheriff muttered as he fought to bring Erika out of the room.

Becky remained quiet next to her lawyer. She wouldn't even look at me. Thank the Lord, because if I had to sit through another outburst, I was going to lose my shit. I wasn't sure how I was going to endure the length of this trial.

On the second day, the victim was identified as Carsyn lee. His wife testified that she had spoken to him just ten minutes before the murder happened. She was in tears on the stand as she testified against the women.

"That was someone's brother, father, uncle, and husband that you took from us. We can never get him back because of them," she stated, pointing directly at Becky.

By now, the sheriff had brought Erika back into the courtroom, where the judge addressed her.

"One more outburst like that and I will hold you in contempt of court. Do you understand, Erika?" he spoke.

Erika just nodded her head up and down and sat back down next to Becky. She didn't say another word. She already knew she was going to prison. She didn't want to say anything else that could do more harm than good.

The news was covering this story. The headlines made national news. Everyone could watch the trial; however, cameras would never be on me. This was for my own protection. The judge sentenced the women to eleven years in state prison.

I knew this was finally the end of this horrifying chapter in my life. I would never see Erika and Becky ever again. NEVER!!

In court, Erika and Becky pleaded guilty, which was part of a plea agreement that reduced the charges from first-degree murder to manslaughter. But before sentencing, the judge allowed victim impact statements to be read. He then asked Erika if she was going to be decent and control herself. Erika responded, "Yes, your honor, I will control myself," in a soft whisper. She knew what the consequences would be if she could not.

After sentencing, the bailiff cuffed both women and transported them to prison, where they would remain for eleven years. They were unable to earn good time for a murder charge.

Chapter 6

Initially, when I moved out to California, I thought this would be the place where I would want to live. While living in California, I wanted to be able to experience different things, meet new people, and everything else under the sun, beaches, palm trees, and different places to go. I wanted to stay busy, but a part of me missed home, especially because that is where I grew up. So, I knew this move back home would be the right thing for me. Plus, Mandan isn't all that big, or even on the grid map, so I KNEW I had nothing to worry about. I was scared crapless of living in California after what had happened to me.

It was just the beginning of winter when Jess and I moved back. Since I did not have a place to live, I moved back in with my parents until I could afford a place of my own. It was a little cool out, about five degrees with a slight breeze in the crisp, cool North Dakota air. I know this sounds crazy, but I actually missed it here. Jess moved back in with her parents as well until she could afford a place. We didn't want to move into a place together until we both had good-paying jobs, which we were both fine with. Her parents were excited for her to come back home, too.

This is where we grew up, a place of unity and familiarity, a place where I felt safe. My parents more than welcomed me back home with both arms wide open. They had missed me. It hadn't snowed in a few weeks, but there were about six inches on the ground, so it wasn't too bad. I had a lot of friends back home that I hadn't seen in years, so after I got settled, we would have big get-togethers at my parents' house someday. I knew it was going to be a day I was looking forward to. When I lived in California, my parents and I would keep in contact, but it wouldn't be every day, and the times we did get to talk were very limited. It was one of the things I regretted when I moved there. But when I moved back, I spent the first couple of nights with family, I had missed them too much while I was gone.

We sat down and talked the first night and caught up on everything. By the time we had moved me in, it was around 6 p.m. Mom made us supper, my favorite: BBQ chicken, garlic toast, and coleslaw. Oh man! It was sooooo good! I can still taste it to this very day. Mom's cooking was always the best. It had only been two years of being gone, but in those two years, I missed Mom's cooking more and more every day.

A few days after I got settled in, I called all my friends and had deep, long conversations with them. I couldn't exactly tell them why I moved back, as all of them asked why I had returned, not until after the court was settled, of course. I ended up having over an hour-long conversation with each of them. They were mad at me for moving away because we were all close, but they understood why I had moved. The only reason I told them I moved back was because I was so homesick, I missed everyone, I just had to come back.

My friends and their parents all came out to visit, as I was also close with their parents, on an early Saturday afternoon, including Jess and her parents. It was one of those cases where my dad went to school with their dads. My mom was from Minnesota; that's where she was born and raised. She moved here for a job. It was a great get-together. Most of my friends got married and had kids in the two years I was gone. It broke my heart that I was unable to see them, but they did send me pictures through email. They all looked amazing at their weddings. They brought photo albums of the last two years, showing what I missed. They told stories, good, sad, and silly. We all laughed and laughed and cried at the sad parts. It was really nice to see them again. I cherished every single minute I spent with them. Time flew by, and before we knew it, it was almost 1 a.m. They all helped us clean up, and then we decided to call it a night and head our separate ways until, of course, the next time we got together, or I would stop by and visit.

The next day, I slept in until about mid-afternoon, then decided to get up and begin my day. I was really shocked I slept in that late. I began applying for jobs that friends had told me about on Saturday. Every day, I applied for about seventeen jobs. It was rough looking for work. On Monday, I went to Mandan and applied for more jobs, and on Tuesday I applied for more in Bismarck. Finally, by Friday, I heard back from one place I applied to on Monday. I went to the interview, and on Tuesday, they offered me the job.

Winter had come and gone, and soon it was spring, turning into summer. The warm air, gentle breeze, and outdoor summer activities filled my summer schedule. My parents had a huge garden in their backyard that I tended for them. I looked forward to summer. I loved eating the fresh fruit and veggies from the garden, especially peas! Every year, I would grow corn, cucumbers, cantaloupe, watermelon, carrots, green beans, peas, pumpkins, squash, zucchini, cauliflower, broccoli, cabbage, lettuce, sunflowers, green and red onions, and green, red, and yellow peppers. It was a lot of work, but I loved every minute of it.

Softball would start in March for practice, and the season would begin in May. I was their starting pitcher, on a great team, and we played as one big family. I had played on the same team as Irelaynd. She was a fabulous outfielder. Softball went from May to August, and we played every Wednesday night. Some days were hotter than others. Those were the days you wished water was constantly being poured on you, 95+ degrees. I remember when we had to play when it was 101 degrees with the heat index. That was miserable. We lost that game, but we didn't care; we just wanted out of the heat.

My birthday fell at the end of July on a Friday, so we decided to have a ladies' night out. After all, it had been a while since we were able to get together. We went to the bar that night and had a fabulous time dancing and hanging out with each other. Jess's parents drove us around, they didn't mind, as long as we were all having fun. They wanted a night out as well, so they joined us.

At the bar, I saw a lady standing by the bar, waiting in line for a drink. I kept thinking to myself, *Man, I know that person, but I just can't pin down who it is.* It had been years since I saw her. I glanced at her for a few seconds and then looked away so it wouldn't be obvious that I was staring. I looked again, and this time she caught me looking. She turned to the barmaid, got her beer, and walked over to me with an angry look on her face. *Oh great, now I'm in trouble again,* I thought to myself.

She walked over to me. "Hi," she said. "Hi," I replied, my voice sounding weird. "You don't recognize me, do you?" she asked. "Nope!" I replied back, kind of snappily. "I'm Raina Lee," she said. "We went to high school together, but I moved after my sophomore year to another town 30 miles south of here."

I sat and thought, *Raina Lee… Rania Lee… who could this be?* "I'm sorry, I don't remember you. Do you have any pictures of us together in high school as friends?" I asked.

She got out her cell phone and showed me pictures. "This is a picture of us at lunchtime in high school, working on homework, a friend of ours took it," she said.

I smiled, my face turning red. "Oh yeah! Now I remember! How are you doing? I missed talking to you. What have you been up to?" I asked.

"Oh, keeping busy. I just moved back here a little while ago. My late husband and I used to live in California, but after he was murdered, I couldn't take living there by myself anymore, so I had to move back," she replied.

"Oh, I'm so sorry for your loss, Raina. Do you have a picture of him I could see?" I asked.

"Thank you, and certainly I do!" she replied. She brought out a picture of her and her husband. "This is Carsyn Lee, my husband," she said.

My eyes just got really wide, and I made a high gasping noise. I couldn't believe it. I had seen that person before but couldn't tell her how I had met or seen him.

"What? Have you seen him before?" Raina said.

"No, but can you send me that picture through a text message, please?" I replied.

"Yes, I can," she said. After she sent the message, she looked up at me, a little confused.

"When I saw your face, Mali, you had that look on it, as if you had seen him before," she said in a concerned voice.

"Oh," I said with a smile.

"I looked at the time on your phone, and it said 12:30. I was supposed to meet Jess's parents outside five minutes ago. I'm sorry to have to do this, but I've got to run. Here's my number, give me a call tomorrow, and we'll get caught up," I spoke, as I handed her a napkin with my phone number on it and then exited the bar. I couldn't tell her exactly how I had seen that face before, as I was sworn to secrecy not to say a single word of what I had seen down in California.

I found Jess's mom and dad outside waiting for me.

"What did you do? Did you get lost?" Jess's dad, Mark, asked me.

"No, it's a long story. I saw one of my friends in there from high school," I told him.

"Ok," he said.

"Mali, get in the car, please. You too, Dad," Jess's mom, Betty, said.

"Ok… ok… ok," I said. So, I got in the car along with Jess's dad, and we were off to Jess's parents' house. I was to have a girls' night campout at her house tonight anyway, but I couldn't wait to show her the picture.

I got my phone out and showed her the picture of Carsyn and Raina. She gasped as loudly as I did.

"I know! I couldn't believe it either," I whispered to her.

Betty looked at us both in the back seat. "Are you okay, ladies, back there?" she said.

"We're fine," we both said at the same time. We just looked at each other and couldn't believe it.

Before we knew it, we were back at Jess's house for the night. The other ladies had arrived at Jess's house as well. It was nice enough outside that we all brought tents and camped out in the backyard of Jess's parents' house. They had a good-sized backyard, so we just camped back there with our own tents. It was just Jess and me in one tent, and Madeley, Irelaynd, and Emilay in separate tents.

We were woken up by the sounds of birds chirping at the crack of dawn and a nice breeze of fresh air running through the tents. We all got up and went inside Jess's house. We were going to make eggs, toast, and bacon for breakfast, but when I walked over to the fridge, I noticed there were not enough eggs, bacon, and bread for all of us.

"Hey Jess, since there isn't enough food for all of us to have the same thing, how about we pool our money together and go get groceries?" I said to Jess.

"Sure, we can take my mom's van," she replied. So, Jess grabbed her mom's keys for the van, and we all piled in.

We got to the local grocery store in our pajamas and sandals and picked up the following items: eggs, bacon, bread, orange juice, milk, and some strawberries. We actually grabbed extra items for Jess's parents as well.

We got home from the grocery store and got to work on making breakfast. We made sure to be quiet since Jess's parents were still sleeping. Suddenly, we heard, "Good morning, ladies!" from Jess's mom.

"Good morning," we all said.

"I see you are making us breakfast," she said.

"Yes, Mom. We are making breakfast for you as well as for us," Jess said to her mother, sticking out her tongue. We just laughed. By now, we were all starving and couldn't wait for the food to be done.

"So, what shall we do tonight?" Madeley asked.

"Let's go out again!" Emilay said excitedly.

"But we just went out last night," I said in a sour voice.

"Oh, come on, Mali, it will be fun! What is the worst thing that can happen, you won't have fun?" she said, giggling.

"Oh, I suppose," I said with an okay voice.

"What time should we meet back at Jess's house?" I asked.

"8 p.m. work for y'all?" Jess said.

We all nodded and agreed, and before we knew it, breakfast was ready to be served.

After breakfast, we went outside to take down the tents and head home for a shower and a nap since none of us had gotten enough sleep. Around 5-ish, I called everyone to see if they were still on for tonight. Jess didn't want to go out, so it was just Emilay, Madeley, and me, which was fine.

We went to a new dancing club in town, and man, was it packed. We had fun, drinking water the entire night, and danced the night away. Emilay left around 11 o'clock, as she was getting tired and had to get up for church in the morning. Madeley left around 11:30. After that, it was just me. I didn't care, I was determined to have a good time.

I noticed a guy in the corner making eye contact with me, so I smiled and waved. He smiled back and walked over.

"Hi, I'm Nephraeu," he said.

"Hi, I'm Mali. Nice to meet you," I said.

"Nice to meet you too," he said. He was quite handsome.

"I noticed you were sitting over here by yourself. Is there a reason for that? Where's your boyfriend? Where's your other girlfriend?" he asked.

"I don't have a boyfriend, and the others had to leave for the night. One had church in the morning, and the other was tired," I told him.

"Oh, well, that's too bad," he said.

"Do you mind if I join you at your table?" he asked politely.

"Sure," I replied. He sat down, and we talked for a good hour or more. He looked at the DJ playing a song he liked, it was a country song.

"Do you want to dance?" he asked.

"Sure!" I replied excitedly. I couldn't believe he was asking me to dance! We ended up dancing the rest of the night away.

Unfortunately, the night had to end at some point. The clock struck 12:20, and the DJ announced it was the last song of the night. He took my hand and led me off the dance floor. We walked over to the bar, and he asked for a napkin. I thought, *great, I got another weird one.*

Then he led me to a chair at an open table. I looked at him and smiled. He smiled back.

"I had an amazing time. Here's my number, please call me," he said, handing me a napkin with his number written on it.

"Call me tomorrow so we can talk more," he added.

"Sure, absolutely! I would love to call you and get to know you better," I said with a huge smile.

He gently helped me with my jacket, grabbed my hand, and led me out to my car. I saw all of my friends out there and started laughing and giggling as they whistled at me. I couldn't help it. He walked me over to my friends, held both my hands, smiled, and gave me a kiss on the lips.

"Talk to you later?" he said.

"Yes," I whispered. I looked at my girls, held the napkin close to my chest, smiled, and let out a little sigh. They started laughing and rolling their eyes at me. I chuckled a little and got in the car, and we headed home. This was indeed one of the most awesome nights out for the ladies, even though I did meet a guy.

Chapter 7

I always thought my life would never change. Moving helped, a lot. I met a man going out with my ladies. He was my height and accepted me for who I am, which, in a way, was a nice thing. It's not every day you meet a man like that. He worked for a computer business that designed programs for children to help them learn how to read and write. My one true love, being with him made me feel complete.

As the year passed by, we went out on multiple dates and hardly fought. If we did have a disagreement, we would always reach a compromise. It was wonderful. So, on our very last date before he proposed, he took me down to the beach. The warm air, the gentle ocean breeze, and I can't forget the perfect sunset. It was sweet and very romantic. I thought it was perfect. I was sitting on a chair when he walked over, got down on one knee, and asked me to marry him. Without a doubt, I said yes. I was so excited, finally, I'm getting married!

We sat down and discussed what we wanted for the wedding. "Let's be different," he said, and I nodded in agreement. "Should we get married on a cruise ship?" I asked, and without hesitation, he agreed. "That's a wonderful idea!" Since he liked green and I liked blue, we decided it would be neat to have a green-and-blue-themed cruise ship. We searched for a few days and finally found the perfect wedding cruise ship. It was white with green and blue stripes. We called the cruise line and booked it right away. The best part was that they had availability on the day I wanted to get married, and we also made sure our closest friends and family could join us.

We saved up our money for ourselves, our family, and our closest friends. We looked into each other's eyes and both said at the same time, "This will be a time we will never forget."

A year went by way too fast. Friends helped coordinate the flowers and decide who would cook the food. Everything was done a few days before the wedding; we made sure everything would be in order when the special day arrived. I knew it was going to be beautiful and wonderful.

As the day approached, it was finally here, my day to marry the man of my dreams. As we were setting up for the wedding, I glanced out at the ocean, remembering how lucky and fortunate I truly was. The day was gorgeous: clear blue skies, open ocean waters, being surrounded by the love of my life, and family and friends. I honestly couldn't ask for anything more.

After the setup, it was time to get ready. I had to hunt down the ship's captain to go over the plans. I wanted to anchor in the middle of the ocean to make it perfect, but when I asked him, I noticed over half the ship was blocked off. I asked the captain what was behind the curtain, and panic started to rise.

"It doesn't concern you," said the captain.

Right then and there, I demanded to know. "I need to know. You tell me right now, or I'm canceling this wedding. I don't want anything to ruin this special day."

"It's a surprise for everyone, you know," said the captain in an assuring voice.

"Okay, phew," I replied quickly. He walked over, gave me a hug, and gently nudged me along. "Off you go now," he said. I thanked him, hugged him back, and proceeded to the wedding preparations.

We all started getting ready, which didn't take very long, maybe a few hours at most. Once we were ready, we headed for the deck, except, of course, me. My soon-to-be husband, friends, and family made sure everyone was where they were supposed to be.

My father came downstairs to walk me down the aisle. He knocked on my door, and I called him in, asking how I looked. He just started tearing up a little.

"Dad, please don't cry. You're going to make me cry, and my makeup will be ruined," I said, trying to comfort him.

I looked my father in the eyes, hoping for some advice, but instead, he hugged me, kissed me on the cheek, and said, "I love you with all my heart. You are with a wonderful man, and I'm so proud of you." Before we could start crying, he grabbed my hand and arm and walked me down the aisle.

As I glanced down while walking, I thought, *I'm marrying the man of my dreams, my friends and family are here to celebrate, and there's really nothing more I can hope for.* I looked up a short while later and met my soon-to-be husband's eyes, and there it was: the spark I remembered from when he first saw me. With a smile, he said softly, "Wow, hun, you look beautiful."

My father walked me to the front, gave me another hug, and kissed my cheek. My soon-to-be husband took my hands, hugged me, and whispered, "I love you." Then he removed the veil from my face, and we turned to the pastor for the ceremony. It went smoothly, and the best part, nothing went wrong. It was perfect!

After the ceremony, the captain had a few surprising announcements for us. I had no idea he was planning this. The first gift was wrapped, and we were all instructed to open it at the same time.

"Ready, set, go," said the captain.

As soon as he said "go," we all opened the gifts like kids on Christmas morning. They were inter-tubes for water. We were puzzled and didn't understand why we received them.

"Everyone, there's a reason why we're giving you these, trust me," said the captain. So we went along with it. The boys received blue-and-white tubes, the girls purple-and-white ones, and the nice touch was that each had our names and initials on them.

The captain made another announcement: "The second part of the gifts is that you all will be able to get free swimsuits and swim trunks in the gift shop two floors down. You will be let go a row at a time."

Again, we were puzzled, but we went along. After about an hour, we all got our swimwear and returned upstairs to wait for another announcement.

"Okay, now that everyone has their swimwear, I want you to go to your rooms, change, and come back," the captain said excitedly.

We all went to our rooms, changed into our swimwear, returned to the deck, and waited for the final announcement. The captain approached us with a huge grin and said, "This is the third and final part of the surprise. If you would all line up behind me, I'll lead you to the final part. Make sure there is no pushing or shoving. There is a spot over there I want you all to go. When we remove this sheet, everyone must remain seated, for your safety, of course! Crew, please go to your designated areas and release the latch when I tell you to."

Then he turned back to us and said, "This is the secret we've been keeping from you." He was smiling from ear to ear.

"Everyone, help me count down from five to one, and on one, the crew will release the latches."

So, we all counted down together.

5...4...3...2...1... and the crew released the latches. I couldn't believe it; we were all in awe. There it was, a giant swim area playground for all of us. There was a baby pool, a hot tub, a wave pool for the older kids and adults. Then there it was, more swim area! My husband and I just looked at each other and grinned. I walked over to the captain, gave him a big hug, and said, "Thank you; this is more than I can accept."

He replied, "No problem. The look on your faces says everything, that you appreciate it and love it."

I just smiled from ear to ear and told him, "More than you can ever imagine." He smiled once again and scooted me along, saying, "Off you go now. Go and have fun on your wedding day."

I turned and walked away, grabbed my husband, and off we went. We tried everything out like little kids in a candy shop. It was great.

The first thing we saw was a huge twisty-turn slide, about five stories high, sky blue in color. We both tried it, one by one. It was amazing, zooming down, then up, then back down again, and right before hitting the bottom, spinning in a circular pattern before shooting out to land almost at the end of the pool. After both of us went, we walked to the next spot, laughing and giggling.

The next attraction was two single slides side by side. One was purple, a straight-down slide with a little bump in it, then another steep drop. My husband wanted to try that one, so I skipped it and moved to the yellow slide instead. This one looked like a series of hills, up and down. I turned to my husband and grinned. "I get this one," I told him. We went down together and came out laughing again.

After the slides, we walked past a lazy river, but we looked at each other and said, "Nah, maybe later." We went back to our family and friends and told them they could try it out. Strangely, they let us go first, which was very considerate of them. Indeed, this was one of the best days of my life. Near the slides and lazy river, there was a small play area for kids, complete with a tiny slide and a little water park for them to enjoy.

Finally, we figured out why we needed the inner tubes we had brought, they were for the upcoming slide and lazy river we had just passed. The next slide was dark blue with maroon streaks. It twisted and turned, but at the bottom was a small pool. People were flying out of this slide like crazy, some even flipping in their tubes! I had an absolutely wonderful time.

At the end of the day, some family and friends invited us to go on the lazy river with them. That's where my husband and I spent the rest of the night. The night was beautiful, the weather perfect, and the captain let us stay in the lazy river to look at the stars. We even did some stargazing and shared a kiss under the stars, it was so romantic.

The cruise lasted a week, but my husband and I agreed to count it as our honeymoon, too. It couldn't have been better. We barely saw most of our family and friends, as everyone was having too much fun. After the week ended, we packed our bags and hauled our belongings off the ship. Before heading home, my husband and I ran back up to the captain, gave him a big hug, and thanked him once again.

We decided to return to his parents' house where we had been staying, at least until we could find a house of our own. Nephreau had wanted a house of his own for a long time. He insisted on house hunting in town but just couldn't find one.

Chapter 8

We spent **quite** a long time looking for houses. It was a tough market out there, too. Some houses were way too big, while others were way too small, but we found a house on the outskirts of town. It was nice: a three-story house, six bedrooms, three bathrooms, a pool in the backyard (which was gated off), and a big backyard. The house was a teal bluish color, with hunter green trim around it.

When we were both shown the house for the first time, we knew instantly we had **fallen** in love with it. We started moving all the boxes into the house, with, of course, the help of family and friends. My vehicle was the only one emptied out; all the other vehicles still had boxes in them. But when I went outside to grab something from my vehicle, I could not find it where I had parked it. We were the only house there, but I came back in and asked for some help. I knew I was tired, but not crazy.

So, my best friend Jessie came and helped me **look** for my vehicle. It was a blue Blazer. Instead, when we came out, we **both found** an RV parked on our lawn with a "No Parking" post where my Blazer had been. The driver had my Blazer towed. Oh, I was furious. By this time, Jessie knew it was trouble. She ran to the house to get my husband, and in the process, my husband noticed Jessie running back to the house. I had been gone a little longer than it would take to go out to the Blazer and back inside. He saw me walking toward this RV.

He dropped everything, dashed out the door, ran up to me, and grabbed me tight.

"Hun, you are not going to go see these people. Wait… whatever it is, it's not good."

I looked at him, tears welling in my eyes. "This jerk towed my Blazer and posted this stupid sign. This is our property, and I'm going to throw him off."

He held me even tighter and said, "No, I will take care of this."

He turned to Jessie. "Jess, go and get one of my good buddies and bring him out here for me, please."

And so she did. He came out, and my husband handed me to his buddy. "Please make sure she doesn't get away. She doesn't put up with crap, and she will throw these guys out."

His buddy held on tight to me, so tight that I swore I was going to pass out from lack of oxygen.

My husband walked up and started talking to the driver. "How may I help you?" said the driver. "You towed my wife's Blazer?" "Yes, I did. You see, this is a campground area, and I posted that sign there," said the camper.

My husband's eyes grew really big. "This is not a campground. This is our lawn, and you cannot be here. You need to pack up your things and leave. But before you do, you need to get my wife's Blazer back, and you will need to pay for all the fees and everything," he said in a very demanding voice.

The driver replied, "I'm very sorry this has happened. I'm not from around here, you see, and I thought this was a campground area. Can you show me where the campground is?"

My husband raised one eyebrow, incredulous. "Yes, but first, my wife's Blazer returned, please."

The driver looked at him. "Oh, yeah, I will call now."

After the towing company brought back my Blazer, the driver wanted to apologize to me.

The driver got out and started walking toward me, but my husband ran out of the camper and intervened. "I don't think that's a bright idea right now. You see, she's really mad at you, and she has a bit of a temper. We just got married, and she wanted this moving process to be peaceful. She's already under enough stress. I will let her know that you are very sorry for this."

The driver agreed that it was the best decision and nodded to my husband. "Come on, guys, let's pack up our stuff and head out," the driver's wife said to their kids.

In order to hold his end of the deal, my husband gave the driver directions. "You need to go five miles north, and at that stop sign, take a right. It's the only stop sign on that road. After the right, head three miles down that road. It will lead you right to the campgrounds."

"Thank you very much," the driver said. "Please tell your wife I'm very sorry once again."

My husband nodded, and off they went.

"Let me go, I'm okay now. I promise… I'll… I will be nice," I said, screaming and squirming.

"Yeah, right. I don't think I could ever believe you on that one," my husband's friend Josh said to me.

My husband came walking towards me but stopped and just started laughing, shaking his head back and forth. Then he continued walking towards me. He walked right up to me, grabbed my face and cheeks, and looked at Josh. "It's okay, you can let her go now; she will be fine," he said to him with a huge smile. After Josh walked off a little bit, Nephreau just looked at me and smiled. "Oh hun, what am I going to do with you?" I just kind of giggled.

He then gave me a great big kiss, and I just went limp… in heaven I was. My husband caught me and just looked at me. Josh had stopped and watched for a little bit just to make sure I would be okay and said, "Wow, I wish I had what you two have." Nephreau smiled and said, "Someday, my good friend, someday!" I am still trying to figure out how he knew to kiss me like that when I was so upset and angry. So, I stood up from his arms and started to talk some more, asking him questions about what was discussed with the RV driver and his wife. But instead of telling me what they discussed, he just kissed me again. Plump, there I go again, weak and limp. This time he caught me and took me up to the house.

I just latched my arms around him tightly as he carried me up to the house. I don't know how he does it, but every time he kisses me, he just calms me down. It's like the whole universe just stops, everyone disappears, and it's just him and me. I sighed and looked at him. "I love you so much," I told him in a soft voice. "I love you too," he said, looking right into my eyes and kissing me again. My friends just looked at us and smiled. They were so happy for us. After all, I have been through a lot in my life and finally deserve to be happy for once.

As soon as he sat me down in the house, the towing company pulled up and brought my blazer back. "Thank goodness that's back," I said to my husband. "Well, I'm glad you're happy it's back, babe," he said.

So, we continued to unpack the vehicles and bring the boxes back into the house. Jess and Josh stayed behind to help us pack until late. We decided to order pizza for supper.

"So, Nephreau," I said, "how did you meet Josh as a friend?" I asked curiously. Josh just started laughing. "Oh gawd, that is never a good sign," Jess said. "Weeeeell…" Nephreau began, dragging it out a little bit, and then looked at Josh. "We met in little league baseball, one summer when we were eight. He was on one team, and we were on a different one. We tied the game, and we got into a little spat on the field. The coaches had to pick us up, and we got put in time out together. We had to apologize to each other and then to our coaches and our parents for fighting. Then we had to explain why we were fighting. In the meantime, our parents were outside the little league office talking while we were inside the office part of the building. They couldn't believe how we acted. We both wanted to win and took our anger out on each other. Nevertheless, from that point on, we became friends. It was weird, but I would never take it back. Nephreau and I have been best friends since then. I wouldn't trade anything in the world. It's not every day you become friends like that in a situation," he said.

I just turned to Nephreau and said, "Well, look at you, turning into a lover and not a fighter," and we all started laughing. He just stuck his tongue out at me, and I laughed even harder.

"So, Amalia, how did you meet Jess?" Josh asked. "Well, it's not as exciting as you and Nephreau, but Jess was playing by herself at recess when I was in the 5th grade. I saw that she had no one to play with, so I went over, introduced myself, and played with her. She is a year older than me, but when she went to 7th grade, we swapped numbers so we could hang out as friends. And from there, we became best friends. Wouldn't trade it for the world."

We continued to unpack. This time we moved to our bedroom, but it was getting late, so we decided to call it a night. "Thank you, Jess and Josh, for helping us unpack most of our stuff. We greatly appreciate it." "You're welcome," they both said at the same time and headed out the door.

"Well, that was sure nice of them to stay and help us unpack," I said to Nephreau with a big smile on my face. He just looked at me and smiled. "What?" I said in a puzzled voice. "Hun, you just can't stay out of trouble for one day. Always busy or getting yourself into some mischievous trouble," Nephreau said, laughing. "Well, I wanted to beat the snot out of that guy who towed my blazer, but other than that, we were busy just unpacking today. I hate when things lay around in boxes and aren't unpacked," I said in a hush tone.

He walked over to me, grabbed me around my waist, pulled me close, and started pressing his juicy lips toward my neck, then moved to my lips. His hands slid up my body to the back of my neck, and he kissed me for a long time. He then grabbed me under my legs and arms and picked me up to set me on the bed. One by one, we took each other's clothes off, first our shirts and pants, then everything else. His muscular, tanned body pressed up against mine, and we started to make love. His hands rubbed all over the top part of my body, and mine all over his. This was a romantic and loving night; we couldn't keep our hands off of each other.

In the morning, I woke up to find Nephreau already up. He came in to check on me to see if I was awake, and I was just getting out of bed when he looked at me and said, "Babe, today I'm going to serve you breakfast in bed. Just sit there and relax. I will be serving breakfast in a few minutes." "Oh, hunny, you don't have to do that," I said happily. "I know, but I want to," he replied. So, I snuggled back under the blankets and waited for him to bring breakfast. "I could get used to this," I said in a hushed tone, but I didn't let it go to my head; I just closed my eyes and tried to go back to sleep. "I will make him his favorite supper tonight," I said quietly. A few moments later, Nephreau walked through the door with my favorite breakfast: scrambled eggs with cheese, bacon, served with apple juice and coffee. It was one of the best breakfasts I have ever had. He sat next to me with his breakfast.

I figured now was the time to mention what was on my mind. After all, we were an open book to each other and didn't hide anything. What was on my mind, you may ask? KIDS! Yes, the 4-letter word. We had been together for almost a year, and I wanted a baby badly. I had baby fever. After all, all my friends were having kids, and I was the only one who hadn't had any yet. I figured I'd mention it to him and see if he'd like it or not. I turned to Nephreau after I had demolished my bacon. "Sweetheart, let's have kids. I mean, we both want them; why don't we try for one?" I asked. He looked at me with a great big smile on his face. "Sure, why not. Let's do it," he said. I was shocked to the floor that he agreed with me. That night, we started to make a family. Weeks went by, and even months passed, and nothing was happening. We both got tested to see if we could have children, and the tests came back abnormal. So, I went in for an ultrasound to see what was going on.

Chapter 9

The ultrasound I had revealed more than we wanted. I had a tumor on my uterus and cysts on each of my ovaries. The doctor had an extensive conversation with me, and I was diagnosed with PCOS (polycystic ovarian syndrome), fibroid tumors, and stage 4 endometriosis. This made it exceptionally hard for us to get pregnant. I felt mortified, sad, depressed, and all alone, but Nephreau took my hand and said, "Hun, you are not alone in this. I am right here along with you."

Nephreau and I talked with our OB/GYN doctor and discussed the best course of action for us. They mentioned IVF or adoption. I'm not against either one, but having a child of my own is very important to me. I looked at Nephreau (or Phrey, for short) and said, "Let's try IVF. Let's give it a few tries; if it works, great, and if not, we can go for adoption." He looked at me and said, "I couldn't agree with you more. Let's do this, Hun!"

We knew this wasn't going to be an easy road. Infertility is never easy, and it's also a sensitive subject to discuss. There would be failed attempts, attempts that worked, and, worst of all, miscarriages. We knew all of this could happen to us; this was what we signed up for. That night, we went to work, found a few places we liked, and wrote down their phone numbers to call in the morning. A few hours later, we gave up for the night and went to bed.

The next morning, we took the morning off work and called four different clinics we had looked at. One was in-state, and the three others were out-of-state. We chose the in-state clinic for now, it was just an hour or so from our house. We felt in our hearts that this was the right choice. We went for a consultation the following week. Phrey and I met with our bosses the next day to discuss time off and maternity leave paperwork. We wanted to try as soon as possible. We had vacation time saved for this reason, knowing this would happen if we couldn't conceive on our own.

It was a Thursday when we went in for the IVF procedure. We went in and came out the same day. Phrey took me home, and I rested on the couch comfortably. Friday, I took the day off just to relax. It would be 16 days after the IVF procedure before we could test to see if it worked. It was a nerve-wracking 16 days. The only people who knew were our bosses, the doctor, and us. We didn't want to tell anyone because if it didn't work, we didn't want to feel like failures.

On the 16th day, I took a test, and it came out positive. We were ecstatic. But knowing this was a high-risk pregnancy, we didn't tell anyone until the end. Tragically, in the third month, I miscarried. I felt horrible, and Phrey panicked. He packed me into the car and rushed me to the ER. That was hard. I felt like it was all my fault, my fault because I miscarried, my fault because I couldn't stay pregnant, my fault in general. I knew this could happen, but I wasn't mentally ready for it.

The following day, we met with our OB/GYN to discuss what had happened. We talked about trying again and decided to wait six months to be mentally prepared.

We decided to try again; I wanted to try again. But I had been hiding a secret from Phrey. I had missed my cycle that month and didn't think anything of it. That night, as I went to the bathroom, I felt something trickling down my fallopian tube and uterus. I got off the toilet and caught it, it was a fertilized egg that didn't survive. I called Phrey in, showed him, and he saw my tears running down my face. We took it to the doctor the next day, and they confirmed it was another miscarriage.

We talked with the doctor and agreed to try only one more time. I didn't think we could handle another heartbreak.

Infertility is so hard on a person. There's so much pressure, you constantly think it's your fault when things don't work out. It's gut-wrenching to go through. Not only that, but insurance doesn't cover everything and often has caps on procedures. Unfortunately, our insurance didn't cover it, so we had to pay out of pocket for this. We ended up taking out a loan just for this last try. It was important that this one worked. It had to.

Friday rolled around, and we went in for the procedure. I took the next four days off, going back to work on Friday, as I don't work weekends. The doctor told us to wait 16 days to confirm if it worked.

The 16th day arrived, and we waited until I got home from work that night, as well as until Phrey got home. I finished work around 5 p.m., and he got home a little after 6. The day went so slowly, and the anticipation was overwhelming. Each minute felt like a lifetime repeated over and over. Finally, it was time to go home. I cooked supper and waited for Phrey to arrive.

He rushed through the door, grabbed me, and kissed me. "So, did you take a test yet, love?" he asked.

"No, babe. I waited for you to get home," I said.

"Well, hurry up and take the test. I want to find out," he said anxiously.

"Oh, Phrey, let's eat supper first. I'm just as anxious as you are, but I'm starving, so let's eat," I said.

I kissed him, patted his cheeks, and sat down at the table. He stood there with a confused look. Little did he know, I had already taken the test while he was gone and planned to surprise him after supper.

We finished eating, and he jumped out of his chair. "OK!! Now go take the test!" he said. I smiled at him. Confused, he asked, "Why are you smiling?" I made him close his eyes, put his hands out, and placed the test in his hands. "OK, Phrey, now you can open your eyes!" I said.

He looked at the test, staring at it. "Is that what I think it is?" he said, smiling broadly. "Yes, babe, it is! It's positive! We're pregnant!!" I told him. He grabbed me, held me tight, and kissed me like no other. He was overjoyed, and so was I. But again, we didn't tell anyone, because of what had happened in the past.

Chapter 10

It had been 11 years since my past had haunted me and 11 years since Erika and Becky were put in prison. Nephreau never knew what happened to me, and I didn't plan on telling him what had happened either. But he called me into the living room and said I needed to watch something. Little did I know it was the news covering the release of Becky and Erika. I had a glass bowl of salad in my hand, and I dropped it, and it shattered on the ground.

I couldn't believe my eyes were seeing this. Had 11 years really come and gone that fast? What am I going to do? I just stood there frozen, and Phrey couldn't figure out what was going on. He had no idea what I had been through. How am I going to tell him all of this? Is he safer not knowing what's going on at all? Am I safe? Are they going to find me? Then Erika gets in front of the camera and makes a statement.

"Hey Mali, wherever you are, I'm going to hunt you down and find you and destroy you," she states.

Phrey just turns and looks at me after I drop the glass bowl. "Hun, what are they talking about, and why did you drop the salad bowl and shatter it? What is this lady talking about, and how did she know your name?" he spoke. I tried to divert the question and started cleaning up the mess I made. Phrey came over to help me clean it up. I started to tear up and told him that I couldn't do this, that we had to move, and that we were not safe here anymore.

He was beyond confused. He looked at me, grabbed my hands, and sat me down on the couch. "Hun, what is going on? How did those people know your name? Are they talking about you?" he said in a puzzled voice.

"Phrey, I think we need to talk. You see, there is a side of me that you don't know. A side of me that once was a wild thing." The look on his face was more confused than ever. "You see, I saw something that I was never supposed to see and got into some trouble. I thought by moving that I would never have to deal with it, that they would never find me, and that I would be safe here," I said in a tearful voice. "I can't go into details of what happened, but know that it was a very bad situation, and that by moving away from California, I thought I left the past behind me."

He grabbed onto me tight and said, "As long as you are with me, you're as safe as you can be." He never did tell me what he did for work, and when I asked, he kept it hush-hush. When it came time for tax returns, he always did them, so I never worried about his job. But little did I know he would be my great protector in all of this. "You will be all right as long as you are with me," he repeatedly stated.

I thought it was a little weird that he said that, but I felt safe with him. He was my safe place. This home was our safe place. Could Erika really find me here? How could she find me? How could Becky find me? I was freaking out and panicking, having a breakdown. I couldn't stop thinking about what bad things could happen.

Phrey grabbed me tight and held on to me until I melted into his arms, stopped sobbing, and calmed down some. He held me close and told me that nothing was going to happen to me, that he promised me that. After calming down some, we picked up the salad bowl I dropped and all the lettuce that hit the floor, and wiped up all the dressing that had smeared across it.

He grabbed my hand, stood me up, and kissed me one more time for reassurance while I was trying to clean up the mess I made. "Let me clean this," Phrey said. "Go sit down and put on a movie. It doesn't matter which one, just put a movie on."

I walked over to the couch, lay down, snuggled in with my blue fuzzy blanket, put on my favorite movie, and slowly drifted off to sleep. Phrey joined me on the couch after he cleaned up the mess and watched the movie with me.

The dream I had was vivid and emotional. It brought me back to the night that Erika and Becky found me. It was like it happened all over again. They were chasing me down and beating me down, and no matter how hard I fought and tried to get away, they beat me senseless to a pulp. I woke up screaming and in a cold sweat, scaring Phrey to pieces.

"What, honey, are you okay? What were you dreaming?" he asked.

I looked at him with worried eyes and told him that Erika and Becky were chasing me again and beat me down to a bloody pulp.

"Mali, you are safe with me. I promise. As long as you are by my side, no one shall hurt you or find you."

Chapter 11

Phrey never did tell me what he did for work, no matter how many times I tried to get it out of him. He just said he worked for the government and left it at that. I didn't press him too much on the topic because he would get a little testy whenever I brought it up.

Phrey went to work one day, and his job notified him about Erika and Becky being released from prison and that Mali should be put into protective custody. His job put Erika and Becky on the no-fly list, so they weren't able to travel by air. It turned out that Phrey worked for the CIA, which was collaborating with the FBI to make sure that the women wouldn't make an appearance where Mali and Phrey were staying.

Phrey called four people into his office that day for a meeting and re-opened the case from eleven years ago regarding what had happened to Mali in the past, disclosing the location of where they were living. He acknowledged the warning Erika had given on the news upon her release from prison and wanted to make sure that the two women would never find Mali again. Phrey was a little worried for Mali, as he knew the chaos that had pursued her before. That's when his job put tabs on Erika and Becky back in California to ensure they wouldn't leave the state ever again.

That night, Phrey went home to Mali, but he knew something wasn't right with her. She was holding her phone up close to her face, holding magazines up to her eyes. It was like she couldn't see anymore. Over the last few months, her eyesight had been declining and getting much worse. When she would drive, she couldn't read the signs anymore, and Phrey knew it was time to take her to the ophthalmologist. They made an appointment, and that week they were able to see the doctor. The doctor ran some tests and discovered that Mali had cataracts.

Phrey was puzzled. "Can they have cataracts at this young age?" he asked. The doctor assured him that cataracts can occur in younger people as well. So they set up an appointment to get the surgery done. One by one, Mali had her eyes treated, and her eyesight returned a month later, but it was a rocky road. Her brain wasn't compensating for having one good eye and one bad eye, so things looked distorted, and the ground appeared uneven even though it was flat. After having the other eye treated, things mellowed out, and she could finally see again. By now, a few months had passed, and she was not feeling well; morning sickness had gotten the best of her over the past few days. But she wouldn't trade it for anything.

Weeks and months passed, and Mali was six months pregnant when she noticed she was covered in black-and-blue marks on her legs, forearms, and abdomen. She had bloody noses on and off all day, was getting lightheaded, and was also bleeding from both ends. Phrey was confused, as was Mali. They went to the walk-in clinic to make sure nothing was seriously wrong, and the doctor ordered some blood work. They wanted to ensure there was no infection and that her platelets were normal. The results came in, and Mali's platelet count was less than 2. The doctor came into the room and spoke with Phrey and Mali.

"I'm afraid that I'm going to have to send you to the emergency room," the doctor explained. "There's not much I can do here. I will call over there and let them know that both of you are coming in."

So Phrey and Mali went home, packed her bags with Phrey's help, and went to the hospital. They had to wait for 20 minutes before being seen, but then they were rushed in by a nurse. It turned out that Mali was in critical condition and needed immediate care. The emergency room doctor explained what was going to happen. She needed immunotherapy and a steroid. They administered a large dose of steroids and six rounds of immunotherapy, but her oxygen level began to worsen. She was put on oxygen and admitted to the ICU for six hours until she could maintain on her own. Then she was transferred to the OB floor, where she remained for four days. After heavy doses of steroids and immunotherapy, Mali was able to go home and be with her husband. Of course, Phrey never left her side while she was in the hospital. There was no way he was going to let anything happen while she was in there. The thought of "out of sight, out of mind" crossed his mind, and Nephreau wasn't going to let anything happen to their precious package.

They went home, and Mali was put on strict bed rest for the remainder of her pregnancy. She wasn't allowed to do much. Phrey secretly hired a friend of his from the CIA, a woman named Lillie. [You initially wrote "Beth," possibly a typo, if it should be Lillie, keep it consistent.] She was hired to watch over Mali, ensure nothing happened to her, and keep her protected at all times.

But there was other trouble brewing that Mali did not know about. That's right, Erika and Becky.

Chapter 12

It had been a few months since Erika and Becky had been out of prison, and trouble had just begun stirring for them. Erika was trying to figure out a way to get even with Mali for putting them in prison. Becky wasn't completely on board with the idea of trying to get even with Mali; after all, they had spent eleven years in prison for what they had done.

Becky soon noticed someone sitting in a car a few car lengths away from where they lived. But this wasn't just a car from the area, she noticed something out of sync. Something was up.

"Hey, Erika, you see that blue car right there? I don't recognize that car, and we have been here for a few months."

Erika walked over to the window and stuck her head out.

"Oh yeah, I do see that car. Let's keep an eye on it the next few days and see if it comes back," she said.

The next few nights, the car never showed up, which they thought was weird. Then, on day three, it came back again. So they decided to go downstairs and check it out. They casually walked by the car, and the guy was on his cell phone, playing a game on it. Erika acknowledged the man, gave him a nod, and walked right past him. He tipped his hat, and they kept on walking.

"Erika, who is that man?" Becky shuddered.

"Don't worry about it. He's my problem, not yours," Erika said.

"Do you know that man?" Becky repeated.

"Becky, he's my problem, not yours. I'll tell you when the time is right," exclaimed Erika.

"You better not be up to no good. I know how you get. You have that crazy-eyed look in you."

Erika smiled at Becky and started to walk up the stairs.

"You know you are going to have to tell me what is up your sleeve sooner or later, right?" Becky said as Erika reached the top of the stairs.

"You will, when the time is right."

All that night, Becky couldn't help but think to herself about who that mysterious guy was. Who was he with? What did he do? What business did he work for?

This certain someone had been sent to keep an eye on Erika and Becky and make sure they didn't leave the state of California. But what Nephreau didn't know was that he was going to be double-crossed and sabotaged. He was going to feed Erika and Becky the information they needed to hunt Mali down and make her pay for what she did, for putting Erika and Becky in prison. He had a secret identity and went by the code name "Lars."

Later that night, Erika went to lay down, and Becky trudged to her room, still sulking over the fact that Erika wouldn't tell her what was going on. At about two in the morning, Becky heard someone talking in the living room. She peeked through her door, hoping Erika wouldn't find out that Becky was listening to the conversation. Lars revealed the address where Mali had been staying back in North Dakota.

Erika had that same crazy-eyed look she had eleven years ago when she killed that person for no reason. Now was the time to get even with Mali. Now more than ever, she was finally in control of what happened. Erika had made plans with Lars on how to take care of Mali and distract Nephreau while taking care of Mali. Becky overheard everything through the bedroom door, which was cracked open.

As Lars was leaving for the night, Becky closed her door softly so she wouldn't be heard, but Erika caught her peeking out of the corner of her eye and didn't say anything. She was secretly hoping Becky would find out so she wouldn't have to say anything herself. Becky didn't see what Lars looked like, so he was still a mysterious man to her. When Becky heard the door shut, she came out of her room, curious about who had been there.

"Erika, was that mysterious man here again?" Becky said.

"Yes, yes he was," said Erika.

"Are you going to tell me who he is?" Becky replied, kind of snottily.

"I'll tell you when the time is right, but for now, the less you know, the better. For now, I will tell you his name. It is Lars. He's a friend, and that is all you need to know," Erika said sharply.

The next day, Erika and Becky packed their things for a road trip since they couldn't fly anymore. They traveled through the states of Oregon, Washington, Idaho, Montana, and over to North Dakota. It took them five days to drive to North Dakota, but they managed to get there. They were no longer being followed by the mysterious man named Lars; he was back in California, "watching" the women at their so-called house.

Meanwhile, Erika and Becky got on the road to stake out the house that Amalia and Nephreau now lived in. They finally pulled up to the house across the street to see what it looked like and what they were dealing with. In the meantime, Mali was resting on the couch, and Phrey was coming home from work. Erika and Becky saw Phrey coming and ducked below the dashboard so they couldn't be seen.

Chapter 13

Mali was seven months pregnant by now, and she was getting pretty big. They found out they were having a girl and naming her Evelyn Rose. They both adored that name, and it was time to get the baby room all ready.

The next morning, Phrey kicked Mali out of the house and told her to go have a spa day. She would never argue with him on days he suggested that. But Phrey would always make sure that Lillie joined her, so he knew she would be protected at all times. Mali went out and got her hair done. She put chocolate brown highlights in it, cut it, got it layered, and then added some curls to make herself look super cute. Then Mali wanted to go get a manicure and pedicure. She got pink, blue, and purple Hawaiian flowers on her nails. Lillie got her nails done too.

Next, they went shopping. They were looking at some baby clothes when Mali looked up and thought she saw something. Was it Erika? She froze in her tracks and dropped the clothes she had in the cart, then looked down for a moment and looked back up. Lillie caught the panic in her eyes and asked what was wrong.

"I… I thought I saw someone," she stuttered.

"Who do you think you saw?" said Lillie, placing her hand on Mali's shoulder as she tried to comfort her.

"I thought it was someone from my past, but I don't see them anymore," said Mali.

It was actually Erika popping her head up, keeping tabs on Mali, waiting for the perfect time to grab her and kidnap her. But Mali and Lillie had no idea that Erika and Becky had been following them around all day long.

Mali decided she had had enough shopping for one day, as she was getting tired and had been on her feet too long.

Lillie called her "boss" to let him know they were coming home. By then, he had the baby room painted and the crib, dresser, changing table, and rocking chair with the footstool all set up for little Evelyn when she decided to make her debut. Phrey worked really hard on it and wanted to surprise Mali when she got home.

"Hun, I have a surprise for you upstairs," said Phrey.

"Oh, do you now? You know I hate surprises, Phrey!" shouted Mali as she stuck her boots and coat in the mudroom closet.

Phrey walked up to her, kissed the back of her neck, grabbed her tight from behind, gave her a great big squeeze, and said, "Follow me." Phrey led Mali to the top of the stairs, put a blindfold over her eyes, and made sure she couldn't peek under it. He led her into the room and asked if she was ready to see it. She shook her head yes, and Phrey slowly removed the blindfold.

The baby room was perfect. It was more than she could imagine. One wall had pink and white on it. The other wall, by the crib, had rainbows on it with a cloud that had Evelyn's name on it, which was perfect because she was their rainbow baby.

Mali walked over to Phrey with tears in her eyes, hugged him close, and kissed him for a while. She loved the baby room more than she could have ever imagined.

But she had to tell him what had happened at the store.

"Babe, I need to tell you something," she said in a worried tone.

"Oh, what is that?" Phrey said.

"I thought I saw someone. I thought I saw Erika at the store, peeking her head out of the clothing aisle. I got freaked out and came home immediately. Aren't they supposed to be in California?" she said to him.

"How can that be?" he thought to himself under his breath. "I have tabs on them in California. This can't be. They have to be in California," he whispered.

"Hun, it's getting late. Why don't you go lay down in bed, and we can watch some TV and fall asleep to a movie?" Phrey said in a reassuring voice.

They headed to bed that night, but Phrey had a hard time sleeping. He was haunted by what Mali had told him.

The next day, Phrey went to work, got on his phone, and had a video call with his co-worker in California. He made him show that he was at Erika's and Becky's house, but Phrey noticed there was no movement in the house.

"Are you sure they are there?" he asked.

"Oh yes! They are here," the co-worker stated.

Phrey went on about his day but still couldn't get the thought out of his head. He asked his wife to meet him at a well-known diner to eat and invited Lillie to join them. That's when he, too, thought he saw Erika peeking from behind the flowers of the flower shop next door.

Phrey was talking to both of us when he stopped mid-sentence, got up, and walked around the flower shop, trying to figure out what he had seen. But when he looked around, he found nothing there.

"That's odd," he said to himself. "I thought I saw someone," he told Lillie.

Lillie looked at him confused. "Who did you see?" she asked.

"I thought I saw Erika," Phrey said.

I looked around to see if I could spot anyone, but I didn't see anyone there. Still, I had this inky feeling that something wasn't right.

Phrey brought Lillie into the store and talked with her while I checked out some flowers I liked. I wanted flowers to plant in my flower bed anyway. I noticed Lillie walk away a little, which was odd since she usually stayed close to me.

"What about these ones, dear? I love them," I exclaimed.

"Anything you want, hun. You pick out what you want for the flower bed," he said.

I picked out some pink lilies and some marigolds. I looked at Phrey and said, "That should complete my flower bed."

"Anything for my princess," he said.

But what Phrey couldn't get out of his mind was that he could have sworn he saw Erika that day, and where Erika was, Becky followed. Phrey decided to fly to California to check on Erika and Becky's house, but when he got there, he didn't find his co-worker at all, nor did he find the women. The house had been empty for days.

A bad feeling settled deep in his stomach, and he knew exactly where they had gone.

To get Mali.

Chapter 14

Phrey tried repeatedly to call Mali but couldn't get ahold of her. Then he tried calling Lillie's phone and couldn't get ahold of her either. He knew it was not good news at all. He knew Erika and Becky had probably muscled their way into the house and were holding Mali and Lillie hostage. Erika and Becky were around the corner, hiding until someone came out of the house.

When Lillie stepped out of the house to take a private phone call from Phrey to check on Mali and see how she was doing, little did she know that Erika walked up to her and hit her over the head with a metal pot outside as she was walking away from the front door. Erika instructed Becky to drag her into the house, tie her up, and put her in the closet. Erika also stole Lillie's gun and put it in her back pocket, where she would later use it against Mali when the time was right. Erika also grabbed the handcuffs off Lillie to use them on Mali later when she found her.

But there was another man in the house, Lars, who double-crossed Phrey and was in the back of the house guarding the back door to make sure no one could get in.

Erika searched the house for Mali, high and low, frantically searching all around the first floor but could not find her. Then Erika searched the upstairs level carefully, being quiet so no one would hear her footsteps as she went up. That's when Erika found Mali in bed, resting. Erika took the handcuffs from Lillie and used them to handcuff Mali to the headboard. Becky grabbed Lillie's phone and took a picture of Erika holding a gun to Mali's head, and the text read:

"If you want to see your wife and unborn child again, you will bring us a million dollars in a case and a getaway car, and never follow us or pursue us again."

By now, Phrey was on his way back in a private jet that the CIA uses to fly in emergency cases only. He was repeatedly trying to get ahold of Lillie or Mali, but neither answered their phones. He called his co-worker, Dewey, who was in a meeting, and asked him to meet him at the house.

Becky and Erika searched Mali's closet for any other weapons and found another 9mm in a shoebox under the clothes in the corner. It had a full clip. Erika gave it to Becky to use just in case someone tried getting into the house.

When Dewey pulled up to the house, he pounded on the door three times and identified himself as CIA, ordering them to open up. That's when Becky shot at the door three times, hitting Dewey in the chest once and missing him by millimeters with the other two shots. He flew backward as the ground caught him. He called for backup and tried to crawl away from the door.

He crawled around the side of the house near the garage and sat against the garage door. He saw the sheriff pull up, run to him, and check for a bullet hole. The bullet had hit his bulletproof vest. Dewey ripped the vest open to make sure it didn't go through, and it hadn't.

"Do you want me to call an ambulance for you, Dewey?" the sheriff asked.

"No, I'm fine, but we need to get into the house and rescue Mali," Dewey said, in pain as he grabbed his chest.

The sheriff called dispatch and requested SWAT to end the ordeal.

Fifteen minutes later, SWAT arrived and took over the situation. The negotiator tried to reach Erika and Becky by phone, but they refused to answer. Then the order was given to take them down.

They snuck through the back door, where Lars was, took him down, and arrested him. Erika and Becky had paid him off to get even with Mali.

They found Becky at the front door with Lillie next to her, tied up with duct tape over her mouth. SWAT ordered Becky to stand down and put the gun down. Becky complied, put the gun down, and was taken into custody and escorted out the front door.

The officers made their way upstairs and could hear Mali screaming, "Please help! Help me!" They could also hear Erika in the background slapping Mali across the face.

"Shut up, Mali. I'm not going to tell you again!" Erika screamed.

The SWAT team slowly crept up the stairs, being careful that neither Mali nor Erika could hear them. Three SWAT members reached the top of the stairs, but one of the boards creaked loudly. Erika heard it and fired three shots toward the doorway, narrowly missing one of the officers.

"Put the gun down and put your hands up," one officer said.

"I will only when Mali is dead," Erika replied.

"Mali, are you okay?" another officer asked.

"I'm okay, but I think I'm having contractions," Mali said.

"Just relax. We'll get you out as soon as we can," the officer replied.

Meanwhile, Mali was still handcuffed to the headboard, and Erika stood near the door, peeking through one of the bullet holes to make sure no one was standing there.

"Erika, let me go. I think I'm having contractions," Mali said.

"Good. Then I can kill you and your unborn child," Erika replied.

"Just let me go. Take the money and the car, and you'll never see or hear from us again," Mali said in a reassuring tone.

At this time, Phrey arrived at the front of the house and saw what was unfolding. He rushed forward, trying to get inside, but the head negotiator stopped him.

"I need to get in there, that's my wife and unborn child," Phrey said urgently.
"I know, and we're handling it. Just give us some time, and we'll get them both out alive," the negotiator replied.

Phrey tried again to move forward, but the sheriff stopped him. "Let them do their job, Phrey. Trust them, they can handle it."

Phrey sat down, buried his head in his hands, let out a long sigh, then looked at the lead negotiator and said, "Okay, I'll trust you, but my wife and unborn child need to come out alive."

Chapter 15

Back in the house, the three SWAT officers remained outside the bedroom door until they were told to advance and take Erika and Becky down. Erika was bound and **determined** to take Mali down at no cost. She wanted revenge for taking her down for the manslaughter **she** witnessed and for sending her to prison the first time around.

"Erika, just let me go. It's not worth it. Let me go, and you can leave here. They will give you what you want," Mali pleaded with Erika.

But Erika was sick and tired of hearing Mali talk, and she slapped her across the face with the gun, knocking her out cold.

SWAT took a tiny camera and put it under the door to see if they could tell what was **going** on in the room, but Erika saw it, grabbed the camera, and ripped it out from under the door. The officers then were **ordered** to take the door down and use a flash bang on Erika, knowing Mali was unresponsive.

Erika started firing the weapon she had back at the officers, and they fired back at Erika, shooting her twice. The officers called for two different ambulances, one for Mali and one for Erika. The officers knew they had to act fast before Erika would pass on from being shot.

They first **moved** the gun away from her so she couldn't reach **it**. The officer checked for a pulse, and Erika barely had one. They tried to stop the bleeding, but it was just too much for Erika. She didn't survive being shot.

The officers **left** Erika on the floor and attended to Mali on the bed. She was still unconscious but alive. They had the **paramedics and EMTs** check to see if she was breathing and alive, and she was. The paramedics loaded Mali onto the stretcher and brought her outside, where Phrey was waiting for her.

He rushed by her side, panicking because she was unconscious. "Oh my God, is she okay? Is she going to make it?" he frantically exclaimed.

The EMT loaded her into the back of the ambulance, where she started to regain consciousness.

"Mali, don't freak out, but you're in the back of an ambulance again," Phrey said.

Mali took one look around and passed back out.

"Mali? MALI!? WAKE UP!" Phrey shouted.

The EMT got in the driver's seat and made a mad dash to the hospital.

Mali was still contracting and going into preterm labor. There, the **doctors** didn't want her to deliver too early, so they gave her some much-needed meds to help stop the contractions, but she had to stay in the hospital until the baby was born to be closely monitored.

Chapter 16

Six weeks. SIX WEEKS Mali has been in the hospital. Mali is so sick and tired of hospital food and is ready to go home, but the doctor came in today and said, "Today is the day, Mali. Today you are going to meet your little one. We are going to take you down for a C-section today."

Phrey and Mali discussed their options between a C-section and delivering the natural way. There had been just too many things that had gone wrong with this pregnancy, and they wanted to be safe and deliver the baby by C-section. The nurse came in and said, "Are you ready?"

"ABSOLUTELY!" replied both Phrey and Mali.

They took Mali downstairs to the surgical unit and got her prepped for surgery, and Phrey got scrubbed in as well. They had been waiting a long time for this day, and now that it was here, they were ecstatic.

Mali was numbed with an epidural, and as soon as it kicked in, the doctors performed the C-section, and beautiful Evelyn Rose was born. Rose was a middle name from Mali's great-grandmother, and Evelyn was from Phrey's great-grandmother. Evelyn was seven pounds, two ounces, and was twenty-one and a half inches long. She had Phrey's brown hair and Mali's blue eyes. She was perfect in every way. She was wrinkled, red, and crying. The first cry was the most beautiful sound we had ever heard. It was proof of life. Proof that we finally made it. Then they whisked Evelyn away right away, and she was not able to be held by Phrey.

After the C-section, they brought Mali upstairs and allowed her to rest. She could no longer feel the epidural, and she had been cut pretty badly and was very sore. Then Phrey entered the room, grabbed Mali's hand tighter than he ever had before, and kissed her on the forehead. "I'm so proud of you."

Then the nurse came in with little Evelyn and handed her to Phrey. Phrey started to tear up and was completely speechless.

Phrey then handed little Evelyn to Mali.

"Hi, Evelyn," she whispered in a crackling voice. "I'm your mom. I have been waiting a really, really long time to meet you."

Phrey was crying. I had only seen him cry one time before this. Not through all the danger, not through any of it. But here, in the quiet hospital room, with morning light streaming through the window, he stood beside the bed with tears running down his face and the biggest smile I had ever seen.

"She has your nose," he said.

I laughed, a real laugh, my first real laugh in weeks. "Poor kid."

"I am serious. Look at her. She is beautiful, just like her mother."

I looked down at Evelyn Rose, our rainbow baby, our miracle after the storm, and I thought about all the scars. The crumpled paper I had become over the years. Stomped on, smoothed out, and scarred. But there was this brand-new paper. Blank. Untouched. A whole life ahead of her, full of walks I could not imagine yet.

"We are going to take such good care of you, my child," I promised her. "You are never going to feel alone. You are always going to know how much you are truly loved."

That night, we opted to keep Evelyn in our room, as we wanted to keep a close eye on her. The nurse came in a few times to check in on us.

"You have a visitor," the nurse said.

"Okay, bring them in, please," Phrey and I said at exactly the same time.

"JESS!" Mali said excitedly.

Jess stopped in to visit.

"I am so glad you stopped in, Jess!"

"Hi, Mali. Hi, Phrey," Jess said as she waved to both of them.

"Jess, we would like you to meet our bundle of joy. Meet Evelyn Rose," Phrey said as he placed Evelyn in Jess's arms.

"Oh, Mali! She's perfect!" exclaimed Jess.

Jess giggled a little.

"What are you giggling about, Jess?" Mali said curiously.

"Remember those nights we would prank each other in California?"

"Yes!" Mali said excitedly. "But what made you think of that?"

"She has your smile, and it made me think of the day we met," Jess said.

Mali giggled too. "Thank you, Jess. I needed that," Mali said warmly.

"Well, Mali and Phrey, I can't stay long. I just stopped by to deliver this and head out," Jess said as she gave Phrey the baby gift and some of Mali's favorite perfume. "I'll see you two later, and take care of that baby."

A few hours later, the nurse came in again to check on us and said, "You have another visitor, and this one is a surprise," she said with a big grin on her face.

"Mom! Dad! You made it!" Mali said through tears as she realized they had stopped by.

"Oh, we figured we would stop since we were in the neighborhood," her dad said.

"Mom, Dad, I have someone I want you to meet. This is Evelyn Rose," Mali said as she placed the baby in her father's hands. "Rose is after great-grandma, and Evelyn is after Phrey's great-grandmother."

Dad was beaming from ear to ear. "You know, we were hoping you and Phrey would start having children," he said as he kissed Evelyn on the head.

"Evelyn is our rainbow miracle baby. She is extra special," Mali said, smiling at her dad.

"Dad, do you remember the story you taught me about the crumpled, stomped piece of paper?" Mali asked.

"Of course, punky. Of course I do," her dad said with a smile.

"Well, Evelyn is our fresh, smooth paper, and she will be protected at all times," Mali said as she reached for Evelyn and handed her to her mom.

"Mom, do you remember taking my sister and me to the park when we were younger, where we grew to love playgrounds?" Mali asked.

"Of course I do," her mom said.

"Well, Mom, I hope you will love the grandma role and take Evelyn to lots of playgrounds, where she will learn to love them just as much as we did," Mali said.

"Phrey and I will too, but we want you two to have a special bond with her as well," Phrey added.

Mali's mom handed Evelyn back to Phrey, and then they left.

"We can't stay too long. We have other things we need to get done," her mom said as they walked out the door.

"Phrey, did you bring that journal I asked you to bring?"

"Yes, hun. It's in my coat pocket, the inside jacket pocket," Phrey said as he was changing Evelyn's diaper.

That night, the nurse encouraged us to let the baby stay in the nursery so Mom and Dad could get some rest. Phrey had to go home to tie up a few work things anyway, and it gave Mali time to journal about her life and everything that had happened in the months leading up to Evelyn's birth.

The next morning, Phrey walked into the room and saw Mali still sleeping. He leaned over, kissed her on the forehead, pulled up a chair, and held her hand as he sat down. Mali heard him and giggled softly.

"Hi, Phrey," Mali said with a smile.

"Good morning, sweetheart."

The nurse saw Phrey arrive and brought Evelyn back in. "I hope you got some rest last night, because today you and Evelyn get to go home. We are very pleased with the progress she made overnight. Here are your discharge papers and a car seat. Godspeed. You have a beautiful family, Phrey. Protect them at all costs," the nurse said.

Chapter 17

Summer had come and fall had come, and now winter was here. It was time for Phrey and Mali to head back to California for some vacation time, but Mali was a little apprehensive about going there again. Mali told Phrey that they should not go for walks outside off the beaten path, but just stay around the hotel. Phrey assured Mali that everything was going to be okay.

"But I have two huge surprises for you, Mali."

She heard a knock on the door, and it was Raina, Carsyns wife who had been murdered. "I wanted to tell you that I am so sorry I was not able to do more for Carsyn and stop the murder. I testified against his killers and wish I could have done more. I am so sorry for your loss, Raina. I know you loved him very much, and I think about him every day and pray he finds peace and that you find peace," Mali said as she hugged Raina.

"Thank you so much for doing that for me and for Carsyn. We appreciate you so, so much," Raina said as she teared up a little bit.

"Raina, if you ever need anything, do not be afraid to call us. Here is our number. I am always here for you," said Mali as she wrote down her information.

"How are you liking it back home in North Dakota, Mali?" Raina asked curiously.

"Right now, it is winter out in North Dakota. January is our coldest month, so we are trying to stay warm back home," Mali said.

"We get a lot of snow during the winter sometimes," Phrey said.

"Well, I just stopped in to say hi and see how you were doing," Raina said.

"I appreciate you stopping in, Raina," Mali said. "You take care of yourself, and if you need anything, do not ever be afraid to keep in touch with us."

Raina hugged them both and walked out the door.

"I wonder how little Evie is doing," Mali said to Phrey.

"She is with your parents, so she should be in good hands," Phrey said to Mali, giving her a great big hug and a kiss on the lips.

They heard another knock on the door. "I wonder who that could be," said Phrey as he had a huge grin on his face.

They opened the door, and it was Lillie. "Lillie!" said Mali in excitement. "What are you doing here?"

"I was here for an assignment and figured I would stop in and say a brief hello. I also brought you some of your favorite flowers. Carnations, Moon Lillies, and Roses," said Lillie excitedly.

"Gee, I wonder how you figured that out. Ne-Phre-aue," Mali said surprisingly.

Phrey held his hands up and shrugged his shoulders. "Gee, I do not know," he said as he rolled his eyes at Mali.

Lillie and Mali both giggled about it a little bit.

"How are you? What have you been up to? What are you doing these days?" Lillie asked.

"Well, Phrey and I are here on a small vacation, but I think he had a hand in that and that it was all preplanned," Mali said sarcastically. "But it was all with good intentions, I have a feeling."

"But we have some news for you that we just learned about. Becky had her case reviewed, and it went to court."

"Becky has reached a plea deal. She agreed to testify about Larbs, the double-cross agent who betrayed us, and in exchange, she received a reduced sentence. She will still go to prison, but not for life," Lillie said.

"I feel like I should write her a letter," Mali said.

"I do not know, Mali. Maybe you should decide against it and let things be the way they are. It will work out in the end," Phrey said.

"Maybe you are right. Maybe we should just let it be the way it is and not contact her or Lars," Mali agreed in a monotone voice.

"Mali, I agree. Just let it be," Lillie said.

"But we have more news about Lars. He testified in an internal investigation, and we confronted him about trusting someone in the company and about how he sold out our family's location for money. This was a violation of keeping us safe, and now I will be more careful in future situations and coverage when protecting employees' families. It broke my heart that someone I trusted broke the trust of the agency," Phrey stated to Lillie and Mali in a heartbreaking tone.

"This did put us in danger, and I hope they put both of them in prison for a very long time," Mali said.

"Mali, tomorrow you and Phrey will go back home and be with your little one, Evie. Here is a gift for your little rainbow baby," Lillie said.

"Thank you, Lillie," Mali said while hugging her.

"Phrey, I will see you back at work on Monday," Lillie said as she closed the door.

"Phrey, I have a feeling we came to California for more than just a small vacation. It was for work too, was it not?" Mali said, looking a little disappointed.

"Yes, it was, Mali. I had to work while we were here, but I could not exactly tell you why until Lillie and I told you what it was for," Phrey said. "Lillie is right, though. Tomorrow, we go back home to North Dakota, and we will have more visitors. But you cannot ask who it is. Another surprise."

"None at all?" Mali said with a smirk on her face.

"None. Now let us head to bed so we can get up early in the morning and head to the airport."

Phrey turned and looked at Mali in the back of the taxi cab. "Honey, I have to tell you something. I do not really talk about it much because it still hurts, but both my parents are not living anymore. They died in a car crash before we met. I just do not want to talk about it because it hurts too much," Phrey said in tears.

"Oh, sweetheart. I am so, so sorry," Mali said as she hugged him in the back seat and gave him a great big kiss.

Chapter 18

We had to be at the airport at 4 a.m. the next morning, as our flight left at 7. "Mali, are you ready?" Phrey asked. "I am so ready to go home to Evie. I miss her so much," Mali said, with tears in her eyes.

Both Mali and Phrey boarded the plane, and they headed back to North Dakota.

Mali met both her parents at the airport. Little Evie saw Mom and Dad and crawled over to her and mumbled, "Mama, dada." But Mali could not wait for her, and she ran and scooped her right up and kissed and hugged her as if Evie was a little pincushion.

Little did Mali know, her parents were planning a surprise party for her when she got home that day. All of her friends were going to show up and surprise her.

Mali fell asleep, so Phrey brought her inside in a hurry, knowingly aware that the party was taking place. Phrey told everyone to get into place.

Mali came inside and saw the pink balloons and the cake, and then all of her friends popped out. Jess, Madeley, Emilay, and Irelynd.

"SURPRISE!"

The entire gang was there. "Oh, you ladies got me! I was not expecting any of this!" Mali said excitedly. "I am so, so happy to see everyone."

"Remember our shenanigans in California? We were giving each other so much flack. So much fun was had, and so many memories were made."

"We remember!" everyone said at the same time.

We all talked individually with Mali and then gave her gifts for having a baby. It was sort of a surprise baby shower that she never got to have. Then some of Phrey's coworkers showed up, and Mali got a little hesitant.

There was a flashback of what happened while Lillie was there and what happened to Erika. Mali dropped her cake, realizing all of these emotions came flooding back. "You are safe. I promise, Mali," Phrey said.

One by one, the ladies disappeared from the party and headed back home. Then little Evie woke up from her nap.

"Let's take a walk," Phrey said, and for a second Mali's head stuttered the way it used to whenever those words came up. But then I looked out the window at the North Dakota sky, painted orange and pink by the sunset, and Mali nodded.

"Yeah," Mali said. "Let's take a walk."

We bundled Evelyn into the stroller. She was almost one now, all chubby cheeks and giggles. The air was crisp, carrying the smell of hay and approaching autumn. Meadowlarks called to each other across the fields, the same way they had called when I was eight years old, learning about crumpled paper on my father's lap.

We walked the road toward town. The road I had walked a thousand times growing up. The road that felt like home in a way California never had. The trees arched overhead, their leaves just starting to turn gold around the edges.

"You okay?" Phrey asked, and I realized I was crying. Not scared crying. Not sad crying. Just full.

"I am really okay," I said, and I meant it.

Evelyn pointed to a bird. "Buh!" she announced, which was her word for everything wonderful.

"That is a meadowlark, baby girl," I told her. "They live here. We live here."

Phrey put his arm around me as we walked, and I leaned into him. The sun was sinking lower, painting everything in warm light, and somewhere behind us was every hard thing that had ever happened to me. But ahead of us was the road home.

That is the thing about walks I learned. You never know where they may take you. The one that changed my life started with a decision to wander off the path, and it led me through eleven years of fear and running and hiding. But it also led me here. To this road, this sunset, this man, this child.

To this moment, which I would not trade for anything.

"Ready to go home?" Phrey asked.

I smiled at him and said, "Yeah, I am ready."

And together, the three of us walked toward the place where we belonged.